EXTRACTS FROM
THE RED NOTEBOOKS

Matthew Engel

EXTRACTS FROM
THE RED NOTEBOOKS

MACMILLAN

First published 2007 by Macmillan
an imprint of Pan Macmillan Ltd
Pan Macmillan, 20 New Wharf Road, London N1 9RR
Basingstoke and Oxford
Associated companies throughout the world
www.panmacmillan.com

ISBN 978-0-330-44954-0

Printed and bound in Great Britain by
Mackays of Chatham plc, Chatham, Kent

Visit www.panmacmillan.com to read more about all our books
and to buy them. You will also find features, author interviews and
news of any author events, and you can sign up for e-newsletters
so that you're always first to hear about our new releases.

Lover of words

Young master of the one-liner

To LAURIE

For ever

Permissions acknowledgements

The cartoons on pages 8 (Nick Downes), 49 (Heath), 63 (Nick Newman), 102 (David Austin), 107 (Heath), 137 (Ivor Roberts), 158 (Nick Downes), 190 (Nick Newman), 197 (W Scully), 214 (Belkin), 228 (Alex) first appeared in the *Spectator* and are reproduced by kind permission of the magazine.

The cartoons on pages 20 (David Austin) and 223 (Bryan McAllister) first appeared in the *Guardian* and are reproduced by kind permission of Janet Flee and Bryan McAllister.

The cartoons on pages 72 (Bill Tidy), 183 (Colin Whelan), 206 (McLachlan) and 257 (Barry Fantoni) first appeared in *Private Eye* and are reproduced by kind permission of the magazine.

Contents

Acknowledgements xi

Introduction *xiii*

ADVICE *1*

AMERICANA *8*

AUSTRALIANA *15*

BEACHCOMBER *19*

THE BLAIR YEARS *20*

THE BRITISH *25*

THE BUSH YEARS *32*

CAPITALISM *35*

COMMUNISM *40*

CORRECTIONS *45*

COUNTRY LIFE *49*

CRICKET *53*

An interesting if not necessarily very useful
DICTIONARY *56*

DRINKING 63

EDUCATION 66

FAME 68

FAMILY LIFE 72

FOOD 75

FOREIGNERS 83

GAMBLING 91

HEADLINES 94

JEWS 96

LANGUAGE 102

THE LAW AND THE LAWLESS 107

LEADERS 112

LIBERTY 123

LIFE AND DEATH 126

LONDON 133

LOVE, BEAUTY AND A BIT OF THE OTHER 137

NATURE 150

THE NEWS BUSINESS 158

Only Connect *169*

Playtime *173*

Predictions *180*

Race *183*

Really? *190*

Religion *197*

Science on the March *206*

Screenstruck *211*

Stagestruck *214*

Television *219*

The Thatcher Years *223*

Travellers' Tales *228*

T-shirts *238*

The Upper Crust *240*

War *247*

Writing *257*

Yogi-isms *263*

The Young *265*

The Laurie Engel fund *267*

Laurie-isms *269*

Acknowledgements

This book was made possible by the enthusiasm of Richard Charkin of Macmillan, who responded positively to the idea in what may be record time: about half a minute. Thanks also to everyone else involved at Macmillan – Nicholas Blake, Jason Cooper, Wilf Dickie, Georgina Difford, Jacqui Graham, Richard Milner and Bruno Vincent.

My gratitude too to all the cartoonists and others who have kindly allowed their work to be used. The cartoonists are: Alex, Belkin, David Austin, Nick Downes, Barry Fantoni, Michael Heath, Bryan McAllister, Ed McLachlan, Nick Newman, Ivor Roberts, W Scully, Bill Tidy and Colin Whelan.

For various other bits of help on the book, thanks to Jack Bannister, Simon Barnes, David Bishop, Henry Blofeld, Charlie Burgess, Stuart Burgess, Duncan Campbell, Pauline Charnock, John Clare, Alyce-Faye Eichelberger-Cleese, Andre Farrar, Michael Heath, Murray Hedgcock, Jon Henley, Craig Hilton-Taylor, Richard Ingrams, Frank Keating, Alistair Kirkpatrick of Silvine, Harriet and Pamela Monkhouse, Nick Newman, Andrew Nickolds, David Rowan, Garry Scott-Irvine, Alison Silver, Marilyn Warnick, Geoffrey Wheatcroft, Theodore Zeldin and all the kind people who have said nice things on the jacket.

The book would be poorer if I hadn't listened to Nigel Rees' Radio 4 programme *Quote Unquote* over the years. (I appeared on it once, along with an actor who never allowed anyone else to speak.) The website *regrettheerror.com* was the source for much of the Corrections section.

My wife Hilary supported the venture in thousands of ways. So, without realizing it, did my daughter Vika. As a family we have experienced more than our share of laughter, love and loss. All of these are at the heart of *The Red Notebooks*.

Since the Laurie Engel Fund started, we have had fantastic support from thousands of people, many of whom we have never met. If you paid money for this, you're among them. So bless you too.

Introduction

In what children call the olden days – 1979, to be exact
– I was on the brink of achieving an ambition and scoring
a job on the *Guardian*. It was the first step, as I saw it,
to becoming recognized as a writer. A writ-or.

What writ-ors did, someone told me, was to write
things down. It was important to keep a notebook, what
some call a 'commonplace book', in which to scribble
anything interesting one saw, heard or read.

Almost every pretentious young journalist embarks on
an exercise like this, I have since learned. My researches
suggest that they normally keep it going for about a
fortnight. Though I am, in almost every other respect,
lazy, disorganized and fickle, I have jotted things down
now for almost twenty-eight years. I think the only other
habits I have kept going so long are filthy ones.

These notebooks are not to be confused with the
normal journalist's notebook, used for day-to-day
newspaper work and then tucked away for a decent
interval in case there's a libel action. I began writing
down all kinds of other stuff too: any quotes, jokes or
facts that made me laugh, smile, sigh, cry, think or simply
raise my eyebrows. From newspapers, magazines, films,
plays, books or conversations.

I did all this in little red notebooks, about which I

became entirely anal and obsessive. The notebooks had to be red Silvine memo books (obtainable from all good newsagents) and I only allowed myself to use a black medium Bic pen (ditto). Since 1979, I must have lost several thousand of the Bics, but oddly I have lost just one of the notebooks, and that was only a few pages old.

Fortunately, both Silvine *and* Bic have remained in business, though early on they changed the cover of the notebooks from a crimson, slightly corrugated material to a more garish scarlet plain card. I managed to cope with this change without therapy.

At first, I was filling four red notebooks a year. And though by the 1990s it had settled down to one, that still meant that by 2006 I was on No. 36 and they no longer had any clear purpose. There was no reasonable way of looking anything up.

I kept going. I nurtured the notion that I might – if I ever had nothing else to do – transfer the contents on to one of these new computer things, which hardly existed in 1979. In the meantime, the books became neater. I stopped using the original combination of longhand and half-remembered Pitman's shorthand, in the vague hope that my son Laurie, who was developing not dissimilar tastes, interests and obsessions, might one day read them.

Then in 2004 Laurie was diagnosed with a rare and obscenely vicious cancer; he died, aged thirteen, in September 2005. One day, seeking solace wherever it could be found, I started re-reading some of the notebooks, and thought maybe other people might enjoy them, and that they could be a way of raising money for the Laurie Engel Fund, which my wife Hilary and I had started in conjunction with Teenage Cancer Trust (see page 267).

After a week locked away, alone with my thirty-six friends and a laptop, the following selection started to emerge. The quotes and facts are, I hope, accurate – and mostly fresh and relevant. Some are poignant and, in our new family situation, poignancy seems to prick us at almost every moment. Most, I hope, are funny.

They are, I hope, a memorial to Laurie who was (his friends all say this too) a very funny bloke. They also reflect what has engaged me for half my own lifetime.

Matthew Engel
Herefordshire, January 2007

Advice

Go your own way, and let the people talk.
Karl Marx, *Das Kapital*, after Dante

There is only one principle of public conduct. Do what you think right and take place and power as an accident.
Revd Sydney Smith

Anger is the most corrosive of the emotions in its ability to increase heart strain. Avoid contact with irritating people; instead write them a letter, then tear it up before posting it.
Dr Graham Jackson, cardiologist, 1998

There are some letters that ought never to be written. Most of them happen to be four pages long.
'Miss Manners', American columnist

Put your money in Old Masters. They fetch a lot more than old mistresses.
Attr. Lord Beaverbrook

If you want to be happy for a day, get drunk; a week, kill a pig; a month, get married; for life, be a gardener.
Chinese proverb

Beware of men who cry. It's true that men who cry are sensitive to and in touch with feelings, but the only feelings they tend to be sensitive to and in touch with are their own.

Nora Ephron, *Heartburn*

Get in, get into the place that's your nature, whether it's running a corporation or picking daisies in a field, get in there and live to it, live to the fullness of it, become what you are, and I'll say to you, you've done more than most men. Most men – and let me tell you, I know men – most of them don't ever do that. They'll work at their job and not know why. They'll marry a woman and not know why. They'll go to their graves and not know why.

E. L. Doctorow, *Loon Lake*

'You know where you have made your bloomer?'
'Where have I made my bloomer?'
'You have let the sun go down on your wrath, it's the
    worst possible thing to do. All the nibs are agreed
    on that.'

P. G. Wodehouse, *A Pelican at Blandings*

If you sit by the banks of the Ganges long enough,
the bodies of all your enemies will float by.
Indian proverb

Never walk fast: you lose dignity.
Winston Churchill to his son Randolph

Love your country, tell the truth and don't dawdle.

Lord Cromer, Proconsul of Egypt, to the boys of the Leys School, Cambridge, c. 1910

Never hunt south of the Thames; never drink port with champagne; never have your wife in the morning lest something better should turn up during the day.

Advice to a son on turning twenty-one, source unknown

— Gentlemen's toilets are indicated by a man in a kilt.
— When entering a railway carriage it is the custom in this country to shake all gentlemen by the hand and kiss all women under thirty on both cheeks.
— You will oblige your chambermaid by hanging your mattress out of the window.

Gerard Hoffnung's advice to visitors to England

Never ask a man if he comes from Yorkshire. If he does, he will have told you already. If he doesn't, why humiliate him?

Revd Sydney Smith's advice to the French Ambassador

'Son,' the old guy says, 'no matter how far you travel, or how smart you get, always remember this: Some day, somewhere,' he says, 'a guy is going to come to you and show a nice brand-new deck of cards on which the seal is never broken, and that guy is going to offer to bet you that the jack of spades will jump out of this deck and squirt cider in your ear. But, son,' the old guy says, 'do not bet him, for as sure you do you are going to get an ear full of cider.'

Damon Runyon, *The Idyll of Miss Sarah Brown*

'Never order thick soup.

'Never read books recommended by rich women.

'Never call a hound a dog.

'Never wear spats with brown shoes.

'Never live in Surrey.

'Never hazard a light observation in the presence of the Scots.

'Never refer to realities in the presence of the English.

'Never forget that on the whole it is more dangerous to do good to one's fellow men than to do harm.

'Never forget that if a fact is not printed on good thick expensive paper in clear solid type the English will not believe it.

'Never drink cocktails.

'Never collect stamps.

'Never forget to assure a woman that she is unlike any other woman in the world, which she will believe, after which you may proceed to deal with her as with any other woman in the world.

'Never motor to Brighton.

'Never take a Pullman train to Brighton.

'Never go to Brighton.

'Never forget that the following take themselves seriously: politicians, vegetarians, advanced thinkers and those in the care of warders and male nurses.

'Never forget that fat men for all their fair, rounded exterior are often cunning and malignant like the rest.

'Never talk when you can listen.

'Never listen when you can read.

'Never read without meditation.

'Never . . .'

At this point the old man folded his pale and finely shaped hands, relapsed into meditation. And soon afterwards passed away without adding any more of his advice. He left two hundred and seven pounds, eight shillings and tenpence.

'Timothy Sly' (D. B. Wyndham Lewis), *Hail and Farewell,* **1931**

If you see ten troubles coming down the road, you can be sure that nine will run into the ditch before they reach you.

Calvin Coolidge

There are the great fundamental truths which of course are serious: there is Christianity, morality, right and wrong, there is no flippancy about these. But in ordinary daily life, perhaps – we learned it as young men more than now – you really don't want to take yourself too seriously. Everyone seems slightly pompous to me now. You must make fun of it, you must make the best of it. Even in war we had a lot of fun . . . and if there are troubles and difficulties laugh them off, and pray that God will help.

Harold Macmillan (aged eighty-nine), BBC interview, 1983

Every man should have a fair-sized cemetery in which to bury the faults of his friends.

Henry Ward Beecher

If power is for sale, sell your mother to buy it. You can always buy her back again.

Ashanti proverb

It is well to know the truth and speak it, but it is better to know the truth and speak to the palm trees.

Arab proverb

You can have vengeance or peace, but you can't have both.

Ex-President Herbert Hoover to President Truman, 1946

Genius is 1 per cent inspiration and 99 per cent perspiration. So you wouldn't want to sit next to Sir Isaac Newton on a crowded bus.

Les Dawson

— Don't write anything you can phone.
— Don't phone anything you can talk.
— Don't talk anything you can whisper.
— Don't whisper anything you can smile.
— Don't smile anything you can nod.
— Don't nod anything you can wink.

Earl Long, Governor of Louisiana

Remember, there are three sides to every story: yours, mine and the truth.

Engel family saying

I got four things to live by: don't say nothin' that will hurt anybody; don't give advice – nobody will take it anyway; don't complain; don't explain.

Edward Scott, 'Death Valley Scotty', Californian eccentric, 1872–1954

Windbags can be right. Aphorists can be wrong. It's a tough world.

James Fenton

Americana

'*You had to bring up gun-control!*'

The only country in history which has gone from barbarism to decadence without an intervening period of civilization.
Georges Clemenceau

The country is good for getting money, if a person is industrious and enterprising. In every other respect the country is miserable . . . The land is bad – rocky –

houses wretched – roads impassable after the least rain. Fruit in quantity, but good for nothing. One apple or peach in England or France is worth a bushel of them here. The seasons are detestable. All burning or freezing . . . The people are worthy of the country – a cheating, sly, roguish gang.

William Cobbett, writing home, c. 1793

Their whole attention seems to be taken up with ordering their lives in a rational way and in avoiding discomfort; when at last they reach the moment of gathering the fruit of so much care and of such long sustained habits of orderliness they have no life left for enjoyment . . . they lack the passions to make one enjoy life.

Stendhal, *Treatise on Love*

Montana . . . It was the world with dew on it, more touched by wonder and possibility than any I have since known.

Film: *A River Runs Through It* (1992)

Before the [Civil] War it was said 'The United States are' . . . After the war, it was always 'The United States is'.

Shelby Foote, historian

Samesville, Samesburg, Same City, Fort Same! Wyoming also. And Nebraska, I have heard said. Some higher,

some flatter, some windier, some hotter. But the same.
Just the same.
J. L. Carr, *The Battle of Pollocks Crossing*

With enough time, American civilization will make the
Midwest of any place.
Garrison Keillor, *Lake Wobegon Days*

Any well-established village in New England or the
northern Middle West could afford a town drunkard,
a town atheist and a few Democrats.
Denis Brogan, *The American Character*

In Britain, you have what we call ad hoc committees:
that's to say, you set up some rules, but if the rules don't
cover your case then it's judged on its merits. Over here
we look up the law on paper, and if the law has
overlooked your particular position, or never anticipated
it, then you're simply out of luck.
US wartime official to Alistair Cooke (quoted in Nick Clarke's
biography)

Ronald Reagan presides over two countries: the United
States, about which he is ignorant, and Movie America,
about which he is an expert. Movie America is a country
that operates within the logic, illusion and structure of a
myth. It is a land of small-frame houses on shady-laned
streets, dotted with good-natured, plucky, quirky white

Protestant families. Individualism thrives. Bureaucracy and handouts are scorned. Large no-nonsense coloured maids occupy all the kitchens.

Jules Feiffer, *Guardian,* **1984**

The American public is almost evenly divided between those who believe God created man in his present form at one time in the last 10,000 years and those who believe in evolution or an evolutionary process involving God, according to the Gallup Poll . . . The findings dismayed some prominent religious leaders who said, among other things, that human existence on earth is much older than 10,000 years.

New York Times, **1982**

I will stand by my own definition of the US as a continental parish for whom the people outside, French as much as Waziri, are remote, inexplicable phenomena, devilish or cute according to circumstance or camera angle, and gradable from debenture holders of high culture . . . all the way down to what are seen candidly as flies on the windscreen.

Edward Pearce, *Guardian,* **1991**

We are Disney and we are National Public Radio, Las Vegas and the Metropolitan Museum of Art, Harvard Square and Birmingham, Alabama, tenth-generation WASP investment bankers and first-generation Somalian nursing-home aides ... Clumsy, corny, well-meaning, adolescent, brainy, aggressive and tough, sentimental and gracious, overly proud, guilty of sin and preaching redemption, we are the people who drop 5,000 lb bombs and food packages on Afghanistan at the same time ... Show me another country that could produce Colin Powell – a Harlem-born Republican with African, Irish, Scottish, Jewish and Arawak Indian blood – and send him to negotiate with sheiks, tribal elders and dictators ... We are exactly the kind of people who drive the religious zealot and the political iconoclast absolutely mad.

Roland Merullo, (US) *Chronicle of Higher Education*, **2002**

The only difference between America and Lithuania, as far as Chip could see, was that in America the wealthy few subdued the unwealthy many by means of mind-numbing and soul-killing entertainments and gadgetry and pharmaceuticals, whereas in Lithuania the powerful few subdued the unpowerful many by threatening violence.

Jonathan Franzen, *The Corrections*

Americans are serial obsessers.

Graydon Carter, *Washington Post*, **2001**

You need never read a newspaper again. I'll read them for you and tell you what to think.

Rush Limbaugh, radio host, quoted in the *Guardian*, **1991**

In America, humour is much less central to daily life
[than in England]. Having a good sense of humour is
like having good driving skills or a nose for wine, or being
able to pronounce 'feuilleton' correctly – commendable,
worthy of admiration but not actually vital.

Bill Bryson, *Mail on Sunday*, 1998

Wanting irony, they [Americans] show each other more
concern.

Alan Bennett

Have you ever been or are you now involved in espionage
or sabotage; or in terrorist activities; or genocide; or
between 1933 and 1945 were you involved in any way in
persecutions involving Nazi Germany or its allies?
❏ Yes   ❏ No

US visa-waiver form, 2006

So now we know a little more about an important
subject: the minds of young Americans. According to a
new survey of 18- to-24-year-olds by *National Geographic*,
63 percent of them cannot find Iraq or Saudi Arabia on a
map, and 88 percent cannot find Afghanistan.

But the outside world should not take this personally.
The survey . . . found that 50 percent cannot find
New York State.

Roger Cohen, *International Herald Tribune*, 2006

Faith is the engine of justice . . . in America as a whole: not the religious kind of faith, but the kind that convinces people that the world is conforming to their idea of it, however much evidence there may be to the contrary.

J. Robert Lennon, *London Review of Books*, 2006

Australiana

The land that foreplay forgot.
Germaine Greer

As *Sirius* sailed past Point Solander, Captain John Hunter watched them flourish their spears at her and cry, 'Warra, warra!' These words, the first recorded ones spoken by black to white in Australia, meant 'Go away!'
Robert Hughes, *The Fatal Shore*

There are only two classes of person in New South Wales. Those who have been convicted and those who ought to have been.
Governor Lachlan Macquarie, 1822

Our duty is quite clear – to gird up our loins and remember that we are Britons.
Joseph Cook, Australian Prime Minister, 1914

They wake me in the dreaming in the dawning of the day
The bugles of England: and how could I stay?
J. D. Burns of Melbourne, killed in France, 1915, aged twenty

The Australian Parliament opened in 1927 . . . amongst those who were present was a black wavy-haired

Aborigine from the nearby town of Queanbeyan, an entertainer who threw the boomerang in return for a coin or two. His name was Marvellous, and when he was presented to the Duchess of York, he took the chance to plead, 'Give poor Marvellous sixpence.' After the ceremony he walked the 10 km back to Queanbeyan where he went to sleep, without a blanket, on an earthen footpath in a back street. The night was frosty and in the morning he was found dead.

Geoffrey Blainey, *A Shorter History of Australia*

Under its general anti-Communist mandate the government sought to encourage what it regarded as right thinking at home and to protect citizens from impure or dangerous thoughts from abroad . . .
In 1934 Egon Kisch, a learned Czech author, came to Australia to attend a Melbourne anti-war conference. The government declared that he had affiliations with Communist organizations and forbade him to land. Kisch jumped onto the wharf, broke his leg and was taken to hospital in Melbourne. The government decided to deport him under a clause of the Immigration Restriction Act which had been designed to safeguard the White Australia policy. Instead of saying openly that a man could not land because of the colour of his skin, this clause empowered officials to give a prospective visitor or migrant a dictation test in any European language. Its obvious intention was to enable officials to

use a language unknown to the testee, who could then be barred – technically on some vague suggestion of his illiteracy. Such was Kisch's reputation for scholarship, however, that the government thought it wise to give him a dictation test in Gaelic, the almost extinct language of the Highland Scots.

Russel Ward, *Australia*

Ah, screw Papua. Next question.

John Gorton, Prime Minister (1968–71), at a press conference

Report on New South Wales Labor Party Conference:
Rod Cavalier, exasperated by the unthinking approach to the debate by delegates, moved that the New South Wales delegates to the Constitutional Convention be committed to reform that would guarantee to the people 'motherhood, long underwear, the triumph of Australian sport, the end of the drought, floods and all other natural disasters, the sun rising in the morning, overseas trips for everyone, and mateship.' This was defeated 2 to 1.

***Sydney Morning Herald*, 1983**

The Australian idea of socialism is paying place money on the fourth horse.

Mark Lazarus, Melbourne doctor

Sing 'em muck.

Advice from Nellie Melba to Clara Butt on touring Australia

The US has Ronald Reagan, Bob Hope, Johnny Cash and Stevie Wonder. Australia has Bob Hawke, no hope, no cash and no bloody wonder.

Roger Wotton, opposition politician, 1984

. . . the usual Australian manner: cursing authority but obeying it all the same.

Hughes, op. cit.

The list of names used by Paul Keating, then Federal Treasurer, to describe Australian opposition MPs in 1984: harlots, sleazebags, frauds, cheats, blackguards, pigs, mugs, clowns, criminals, stupid foul-mouth grub, corporate crook, rustbucket, scumbag, rip-off merchants, constitutional vandals, perfumed gigolos, gutless spiv, stunned mullets, barnyard bullies, piece of criminal garbage.

Sydney Morning Herald, **1985**

JULIA GILLARD: (Labor front-bencher): Mr Speaker, I move that that snivelling grub over there be no further heard.
SPEAKER: The Manager of Opposition Business will withdraw that.
GILLARD: If I have offended grubs I withdraw unconditionally.

Exchange in Federal Parliament, 2006

Beachcomber

Characters invented by J. B. Morton, author of the 'Beachcomber' column in the *Daily Express*, 1924–75 include:

The Khur of Kashdown and Getaweh

Bakrasha the Egyptian irredentist

Hight, the M'Bakwa of M'Gonkawiwi

The three Scots sportsman-drinkers:
    the Macaroon of Macaroon,
    the Laird of Kilcockrobbin,
    the Marquess of Lochstoch and Barrell

Vita Brevis

Big White Carstairs

The Harbour-master of Grustiwowo Bay

Mr Justice Cocklecarrot

Captain Foulenough

Dr Strabismus (whom God preserve) of Utrecht, inventor
    of the leather grape, the revolving wheelbarrow,
    a hollow glass walking stick for keeping very small
    flannel shirts in, waterproof onions, a bottle with
    its neck in the middle, false teeth for swordfish and
    a foghorn sharpener.

The Blair Years

His air of haughty incredulity, like a llama surprised in the bath, was well worth waiting up for.

Nancy Banks-Smith, on the Portillo moment at the 1997 election,
Guardian

In a sense, Tony Blair is like Fortinbras, the character with the best timing in all Shakespeare. He comes on in Act V, Scene 2, of *Hamlet* to find an army of dead and dying main characters and, not surprisingly, says that he is taking over. The last Tory government was, anyway, a bit like *Hamlet*, with a decent, dithering lead, any number of untrustworthy courtiers, a ghost (female) who kept barging in, and the Tory Party herself cast in the role of Ophelia, floating downstream, chanting snatches of old songs, before being dragged under, drowned, and given a bad-tempered funeral.

Robert Maclennan MP, President of the Liberal Democrats, 1997

Sooner or later, such a man hangs himself: but when given rope, not stick. MPs can only give stick. Time will give him rope.

Matthew Parris on Alastair Campbell facing the Commons public administration committee, *The Times*, 1998

The problem with Cool Britannia is that it was a party to which our people weren't invited.

Anonymous Labour MP, quoted in *The Times*, 1998

The best definition of the Third Way is whatever Blair actually does.

Ralf Dahrendorf, *Foreign Affairs*, 1999

A lesson Blair learned from the Thatcherites was that, in order to control the debate, you must command the language in which it is conducted. By casting himself as modern, moderate and dynamic, he painted his opponents, whether they be to the left or to the right, as antiquated, extreme and obsolete.

Andrew Rawnsley, *Servants of the People*

In the Labour Party magazine it was announced that 'Tony's favourite food is fish and chips. He gets a takeaway from his local chippy whenever he is at home in his constituency.' In the *Islington Cookbook* his favourite food was 'fresh fettuccine garnished with an exotic sauce of olive oil, sun-dried tomatoes and capers'.

William Hague, 2002

MR TONY MCWALTER (Hemel Hempstead): My right hon. friend is sometimes subject to rather unflattering or even malevolent descriptions of his motivation. Will he provide the House with a brief characterisation of the political philosophy that he espouses and which underlies his policies?

HON. MEMBERS: Hear, hear.

THE PRIME MINISTER: First, I should thank my hon. friend for his question, which has evinced such sympathy in all parts of the House, about the criticism of me. The best example that I can give is the rebuilding of the National Health Service today under this Government – extra investment. For example, there is the appointment today of Sir Magdi Yacoub to head up the fellowship scheme that will allow internationally acclaimed surgeons and consultants from around the world to work in this country. I can assure the House and the country that that extra investment in our NHS will continue under this Government. Of course, it would be taken out by the Conservative party.

Hansard, 27 February 2002

What are the principles of foreign policy that should guide us? First we should remain the closest ally of the US, and as allies influence them to continue broadening their agenda ... the price of influence is that we do not leave the US to face the tricky issues alone.

Blair to meeting of Britain's ambassadors, January 2003

There is nothing more calculated to impair the judgement of a British prime minister than a standing ovation from both Houses of Congress.

Sir Geoffrey Howe, 2004

Policy-driven evidence-making ...

Philip Stephens, *Financial Times*, 2006

Some time before Mr George Bush's bout of disrespectful Texan familiarity – 'Yo, Blair' – a member of the government addressed the Prime Minister by his surname alone. It was Lord Irvine of Lairg. 'Where's the whisky, then, young Blair?' the Lord Chancellor asked of his former pupil at the Bar. Mr Tony Blair's response is not recorded. Like most power-maniacs, he is uninterested in food or drink. But soon afterwards Lord Irvine was replaced on the Woolsack . . .

Alan Watkins, *Independent on Sunday*, 2006

I had absolutely no expectations of Tony Blair, and even I have been disappointed.

Linda Smith

There has been a lot more sunshine since people voted Labour in 1997.

Jack Straw, to the House of Commons, 2006

The British

England . . . the land of embarrassment and breakfast.
Julian Barnes, *Flaubert's Parrot*

When London is nothing more than a memory, and the Old Bailey has sunk back into the primeval mud, my country will be remembered for three things: the British breakfast, *The Oxford Book of English Verse*, and the presumption of innocence.
John Mortimer, *Rumpole of the Bailey*

If a man dies in India, the woman flings herself on the funeral pyre. If a man dies in England, the woman goes into the kitchen and says: 'Seventy-two baps, Connie. You slice, I'll spread.'
Victoria Wood

Your average Frenchie. Magnificent coq au vin, come the hostilities, bashes off to Vichy. Eyeties. Tanks with four gears, all reverse. Pasta magnifico. English, spotted dick and watery greens. Fight till they drop. Reason: nothing to live for.
David Nobbs, *The Fall and Rise of Reginald Perrin*

We're conceived in irony. We float in it from the womb. It's the amniotic fluid. It's the silver sea. It's the waters at their priest-like task, washing away guilt and purpose and responsibility. Joking but not joking. Caring but not caring. Serious but not serious.

Alan Bennett, *The Old Country*

I'm not the best conductor in the country. On the other hand I'm better than any damn foreigner.

Sir Thomas Beecham

. . . that pale English dawn light which comes on like a wan bureaucrat to give notice that the day ahead will once again be one of low horizons and modest expectations.

Christopher Hope, *Kruger's Alp*

British lager is an imitation Continental beer drunk by refined ladies, people with digestive ailments, tourists and other weaklings.

***Süddeutsche Zeitung*, Munich, c. 1979**

Marmite, fish and sex.

The three things hostage Roger Cooper missed while held captive in Iran, *Guardian*, 1993

If you eliminate smoking and gambling, you will be amazed to find that almost all an Englishman's pleasures can be, and mostly are, shared by his dog.

George Bernard Shaw

In 1939 Mrs Slack moved into a council house in Browning Road, Sheffield. The gas people were to disconnect her gas cooker and bring it from her old home to her new one. But the cooker never moved. For twenty years Mrs Slack, now sixty-eight, waited. For twenty years she cooked on a coal fire. She explains: 'My husband Joe was a quiet man. He didn't like making a fuss.'

Sunday Pictorial, 1959, quoted by Hugh Cudlipp in *At Your Peril*

The London chattering classes know more about South Africa than Scotland.

Andrew Neil

FOGGY: Yorkshire is not even one of the superpowers
    competing for the ideological leadership of the world.
CLEGG: It all went wrong when they sacked Boycott.

Roy Clarke, *Last of the Summer Wine*

. . . The tinkle of the hammer on the anvil in the country smithy, the corncrake on a dewy morning, the sound of the scythe against the whetstone, and the sight of the plough team coming over the brow of the hill.

Stanley Baldwin, 1924

. . . Long shadows on county cricket grounds, warm beer, invincible green suburbs, dog-lovers and old maids bicycling through the morning mist.

John Major, 1993

... the diversity of it, the chaos! The clatter of clogs
in the Lancashire mill towns, the to-and-fro of lorries on
the Great North Road, the queues outside the Labour
Exchanges, the rattle of pin-tables in Soho pubs, the old
maids biking to Holy Communion through the mists of
the autumn morning – all these are not only fragments,
but characteristic fragments, of the English scene.
How can one make a pattern out of this muddle?

George Orwell, *The Lion and the Unicorn* (1941)

The alternative to expansion is not, as some occasionally
seem to suppose, an England of quiet market towns
linked only by trains puffing slowly and peacefully
through green meadows. The alternative is slums,
dangerous roads, old factories, cramped schools, stunted
lives.

Ted Heath, 1973

Wales now has more people employed in television and
film than in coal.

***Sunday Times*, 1992**

... 'typical' was regarded as such an unfair word in
England. And yet there *was* such a thing as typical on
the coast – but to an alien something typical could seem
just as fascinating as the mosques of the Golden Horn.
There was always an Esplanade, and always a Bandstand
on it; always a War Memorial and a Rose Garden and a

bench bearing a small stained plaque that said, To the Memory of Arthur Wetherup . . . There was now a parking lot where the Romans had landed. The discotheque was called Spangles. The Museum was shut that day, the Swimming Pool was closed for repairs, the Baptist church was open, there were nine motor coaches parked in front of the broken boulders and ruined walls called The Castle. At the café near the entrance to The Castle a fourteen-year-old girl served tea in cracked mugs, and cellophane-wrapped cookies, stale fruitcake and cold pork pies. She said, 'We don't do sandwiches,' and, 'We're all out of spoons' . . . The railway had been closed down in 1964, and the fishing industry had folded five years ago. The art-deco cinema was now a bingo hall and what had been a ship's chandler was now The Cinema Club, where Swedish pornographic films were shown all day (Members Only) . . . A nuclear power station quaintly named Thorncliffe was planned for the near future a mile south of The Cobbler. Bill Haley and his Comets had once sung at The Lido. The new shopping precinct was a failure. The new bus shelter had been vandalised. It was famous for its whelks. It was raining.

Paul Theroux, *The Kingdom by the Sea*

More than two-thirds of people do not take part in any community activity and half say they would never even pass the time of day with a stranger in a local shop, according to research from the Royal Society for Arts.

It described the social isolation experienced by most adults as 'community detachment syndrome'. A third of people know more than ten of their neighbours by name, but 82 per cent would not strike up a conversation at the school gates, it said.

Guardian, 2006

BANBURY was the most Puritan English town in the seventeenth century; BICKLEIGH BRIDGE, Devon, is alleged to be the inspiration for 'Bridge Over Troubled Water'; BRIDGNORTH, Shropshire, 'is the ideal-sized town . . . large enough to be varied and interesting but small enough for the locals to know which of the traffic wardens is the most vindictive' (David McKie, Guardian, 1999); the church and priory at CARTMEL still places a fresh loaf every Sunday on a shelf in case any of the parish poor have need of it; seven thousand Indian ring-necked parakeets who formed a colony by the rugby ground in ESHER, disappeared in 2006 as mysteriously as they arrived; the Scottish island of FOULA celebrates Christmas on 6 January, taking no account of the 1752 switch to the Gregorian calendar; for the same reason New Year's Day is celebrated on 13 January, in the GWAUN VALLEY, Pembrokeshire; there is a Welsh-language school in HARLESDEN, North London; people are believed to have lived in caves at KINVER, Staffordshire, from the Stone Age until the 1960s; LEEK, Staffordshire, has a 'double sunset': if you stand in the old churchyard at dusk, the sun will set behind a hill, partially reappear and set again behind the Cheshire plain – though not as clearly now as before due to new trees; NEWTON ABBOT in Devon has large numbers of pied wagtails; NEWTON STEWART, Scotland, and WARRINGTON were reported in 1997 to have the highest concentration of pubs in the UK while SOUTHEND-ON-SEA had the fewest (due to the local influence of the Salvation Army); posters for the Wallace and Gromit film Curse of the Were-Rabbit were banned from PORTLAND, Dorset because rabbits are locally considered to be bad luck (their burrowing causes landslides in the Portland stone quarries) – the word is taboo and locals refer to 'underground mutton' or 'furry things'; the last remaining Temperance bar (selling sarsaparilla and blood beer) is Fitzpatrick's, RAWTENSTALL; RUGELEY, Staffordshire, wanted to change its name in 1855 because of the publicity received by 'the Rugeley poisoner', William Palmer – they were said to have changed their minds when the Prime Minister, Lord Palmerston, said they would have to name it after him instead; there is a Lenin Terrace in Stanley, Co. Durham (and a Kremlin Drive in LIVERPOOL, a Stalin Road in COLCHESTER and a Gagarin Way in LUMPHINNANS, Fife); THETFORD, Norfolk, is the lightning capital of Britain; a plaque at WIDNES railway station says Paul Simon composed 'Homeward Bound' there, but locals say he must have written it at now-demolished Widnes Central, and Simon was quoted in 2006 as saying it was written in a hotel room.

The Bush Years

You win some, you lose some and then there is this little-known third category . . .
Al Gore

Our long national nightmare of peace and prosperity is finally over . . . We must squander our nation's hard-won budget surplus on tax breaks for the wealthiest 15 per cent. And, on the foreign front, we must find an enemy and defeat it.
Satirical magazine *The Onion* suggesting an inaugural address for George W. Bush, January 2001

Throughout the twentieth century, small groups of men seized control of great nations, built armies and arsenals, and set out to dominate the weak and intimidate the world.
George W. Bush's real State of the Union address, January 2003

The best way to get the news is from objective sources. And the most objective sources I have are people on my staff.
Bush, quoted in the *New York Times*, 2003

It's not true, it's not true, it's not true, nothing can be done about it.

Administration policy on global warming according to Paul Krugman,
***New York Times*, 2002**

Conservative activists came to Washington to do good and stayed to do well.

***Weekly Standard*, 2005**

I believe this was not an act of desperation, but an act of asymmetrical warfare waged against us.

Rear Admiral Harry Harris, camp commander, on three suicides by prisoners at Guantánamo Bay, quoted in the *Guardian*, 2006

I convince myself each day that you guys are all subhuman – agents of the devil – so that I can do my job. Otherwise I'd have to treat you like humans, and we don't do this to people where I come from.

US guard at Bagram, Afghanistan, quoted by detainee Moazzam Begg, *Enemy Combatant*

This presidency never had a vision for the world. It instead had an idée fixe about one country, Iraq, and in pursuit of that obsession recklessly harnessed American power to gut-driven improvisation and PR strategies, not doctrine.

Frank Rich, *New York Times*, 2006

How long does it take you to get home? Eight hours? Me too! Russia is a big country! Hey, it takes him eight hours to fly home. Eight hours! Russia's big and so is China!

Bush to Hu Jintao of China at the St Petersburg G8 summit, 2006

George Bush hasn't got a clue what he's doing. He asked me what state Wales was in. I said, 'It's its own country next to England, Mr Bush.' I thought, 'You twat.'

Charlotte Church, Welsh singer

At a reception following the 2006 midterm election, President Bush approached Senator-elect James Webb, Democrat from Virginia. 'How's your boy?' asked Mr Bush.

'I'd like to get them out of Iraq, Mr President,' replied Mr Webb, whose son, a Marine lance corporal, is risking his life in Mr Bush's war of choice.

'That's not what I asked you,' the president snapped. 'How's your boy?'

'That's between me and my boy, Mr President,' said Mr Webb.

Quoted by Paul Krugman, *New York Times*, December 2006

Capitalism

Advertising is not a new thing. We think of the stained-glass windows in Chartres Cathedral as art, but when they were made they were art only incidentally. They were put there to sell theology – they were billboards – and if the people who built the cathedral had had neon they would have gone crazy for it. There's nothing new about any of this. The mosaics in Byzantine churches and early Christian churches are billboards selling Christianity. Tiepolo's ceilings are Counter-Reformation propaganda. Selling is an old tradition, and we can learn from it.

Robert Venturi, architect, *New Yorker*, 1999

The two infallible powers. The Pope and Bovril.

Advertising slogan, c. 1890

The consumer is not a moron. She is your wife.

David Ogilvy, advertising executive

The [South Sea] Company was valued at more than £300 million, the equivalent of many billions of dollars today and ten times the size of the debt it was holding. Yet its ships had not sailed anywhere near the South Seas. Truly, the country had gone mad.

Malcolm Balen, *The Secret History of the South Sea Bubble*

Things that can't go on forever, don't.

Stein's Law, attr. Herb Stein, Nixon's chief economic adviser

I once went into Manchester with such a bourgeois, and spoke to him of the bad, unwholesome method of building, the frightful condition of the working-people's quarters, and asserted that I had never seen so ill-built a city. The man listened quietly to the end, and said at the corner where we parted: 'And yet there is a great deal of money made here, good morning, sir.'

Friedrich Engels, *The Condition of the Working Class in England*, 1845

During a visit to Tokyo in the early 1950s, John Foster Dulles [US Secretary of State] appealed to the Japanese to make greater efforts to export to the United States. There were, he said, promising export opportunities in pyjamas and table napkins.

***Daily Telegraph*, 1988**

One OECD economist claimed that the whole problem of the 1970s really had its origins in the failure of the Peruvian anchovy catch in the late sixties. Anchovies were an important source of fishmeal for feeding cattle. The increase in the price of feed pushed up beef prices; this fed through to general inflation; and this precipitated the oil-price rise by the OPEC countries. *Hinc illae lacrimae.*

P. P. McGuinness, *Australian*, 1990

A Texan chicken magnate, Lonnie 'Bo' Pilgrim, walked onto the floor of the State Senate and handed $10,000 cheques to several legislators during the debate on a bill about compensating workers for job injuries. This was legal in Texas though the fuss prompted most of the recipients to return the money, generally after they cashed the cheques.

The Economist, 1991

In the history of the world, no one ever washed a rented car.

Lawrence Summers, former US Treasury Secretary

We cannot trust some people who are nonconformists . . . we will make conformists out of them in a hurry . . . The organization cannot trust the individual; the individual must trust the organization.

Ray Kroc, founder of McDonald's

An oil prospector died and went to heaven. He asked St Peter for a place, but was told there was no more room because there were already too many oil prospectors there. 'Do you mind if I say four words?' 'OK.' 'Oil discovered in hell!' he cried. The prospectors all fled and St Peter invited him in. 'No, I think I'll go along with the rest of the boys. There may be some truth to the rumour.'

Warren Buffett, quoted in the *New Yorker*, 1999

Two rival shoe salesman find themselves in Africa. The first salesman wires back to Head Office: 'No prospect of sales. No one wears shoes here.' The other one wires: 'No one wears shoes here. Send all possible stock – we can dominate the market.'

Akio Morita, co-founder of Sony, quoted in the *Daily Mail*, 1987

I keep hearing 'Feed the poor, clothe the hungry, give shelter to those who don't have it'. The bozos that say this don't recognize that capitalism and technology have done more to feed and clothe and shelter and heal people than all the charity and church programmes in history. So they preach about it, and we are the ones doing it. They rob Peter to pay Paul, but they always forget that Peter is the one creating the wealth in the first place.

T. J. Rodgers, chief executive of Cypress Semi-Conductor, *New York Times*, 2001

Naming consultants have an urban folklore all their own, full of the classic mistranslation nightmares that haunt their sleep: the Nova car, meaning 'doesn't go' in Spanish markets; likewise the Pinto, found to refer to tiny male genitals in Brazilian slang; and the cola slogan 'Come Alive with Pepsi', supposedly translated into Chinese as 'Pepsi: Brings Your Ancestors Back From The Dead'. 'I remember one we did recently where we chose the

name, and we were happy with it . . . until we discovered
that in one of the key markets, Poland, it meant
"armpit smell".'

Guardian, 2001

Communism

It will not even pay for the cigars I smoked writing it.
Karl Marx on *Das Kapital*

Marx and Engels refused their support to the British
Marxist Party. In no other country did this occur, and the
cause was wholly personal. 'England For All' was in part
an exposition of Marx's views, but H. M. Hyndman had
not acknowledged Marx by name.
G. D. H. Cole and Raymond Postgate, *The Common People*

ALEXANDER KERENSKY (Menshevik leader): You Bolsheviks
    recommend childish prescriptions – arrest, kill,
    destroy. What are you – socialists or police of the old
    regime?
LENIN (to the chairman): You should call him to order.
First all-Russian Congress of Soviets, June 1917

He does what needs doing and doesn't make a hobby of
his soul.
Lenin on Stalin in *State of Revolution* by Robert Bolt

There is really nothing more delightful than carefully
plotting the trap into which your enemy is bound to fall
and then going to bed.
Stalin, quoted in *The Economist*, 1991

If you don't shut your mouth, we'll get the Party a new Lenin's widow.

Stalin to Nadezhda Krupskaya

It's quite clear – it's got to look democratic, but we must have everything in our control.

Walter Ulbricht, East German leader, 1945

During McCarthyism, a Warner Brothers employee protested to Harry Warner that he was an anti-Communist. 'I don't give a shit what kind of Communist you are. Get outta here.'

Guardian, 1989

It was officially announced that in 1958 China's wheat output had overtaken that of the United States. The Party newspaper, the *People's Daily*, started a discussion on the topic 'How do we cope with the problem of producing too much food?'

Jung Chang, *Wild Swans*

As the sixties began, a great famine spread across China. In Chengdu, the monthly food ration for each adult was reduced to nineteen pounds of rice, 3.5 ounces of cooking oil, and 3.5 ounces of meat, when there was any. Scarcely anything else was available, not even cabbage. Many people were afflicted by edema, a condition in which fluid accumulates under the skin because of malnutrition. The patient turns yellow and swells up. The most popular remedy was eating chlorella, which was supposed to be rich in protein. Chlorella fed on human urine, so people stopped going to the toilet and peed into spittoons instead, then dropped the chlorella seeds in; they grew into something looking like green fish roe in a couple of days, and were scooped out of the urine, washed, and cooked with rice. They were truly disgusting to eat, but did reduce the swelling.

Ibid.

This year will be harder than last year. It will, however, be easier than next year.

Albanian leader Enver Hoxha's New Year message, 1967

Q: Did Albania's Communists make any mistakes?
FATMIR QUMBARA, party official: We shouldn't have
    collectivized livestock in 1978.

Interview with the *Wall Street Journal*, 1991

A short list of epithets officially approved by [the Romanian dictator] Ceauşescu for use in accounts of his achievements would include: The Architect; The Creed-shaper; The Wise Helmsman; The Tallest Mast; The Nimbus of Victory; The Visionary; The Titan; The Son of the Sun; A Danube of Thought; The Genius of the Carpathians.

Tony Judt, *Post-War*

On to Full Cost Accounting!
Chapter heading, Mikhail Gorbachev, *Perestroika*

That was how people lost faith in Communism, she said, how it collapsed at grass-roots – not through philosophic doubt or horror at Stalin, but because a local party minion had purloined funds or wangled a holiday on the Black Sea.
Colin Thubron, *In Siberia*

The simple fact is that the Soviet Union was unable to prevent its citizens from learning about the West and it was obvious from the way the young of Moscow dressed, and from the music they played, that they considered life abroad better than what they had at home. The media, not the spies, won the Cold War . . . MI5, Britain's so-called crack counter-espionage service, never caught a single spy on its own during the whole fifty years.
Philip Knightley, *A Hack's Progress*

Everything was For Ever, Until it was No More: The Last Soviet Generation
Book by Alexei Yurchak, 2005

All nine members of the [Chinese] Communist Party's all-powerful Standing Committee of the Politburo were trained as engineers, and their faith in the power of man over nature remains unshaken.
***Washington Post*, June 2003**

Capitalism with a Stalinist face.

Grigory Yavlinsky, Russian liberal, on the Putin regime

The Soviet police was beyond the reach of time and history. It was protean. *That* was its secret. The Cheka had become the GPU, and then the OGPU, and then the NKVD, and then the NKGB and then the MGB, and then the MVD and finally the KGB: the highest stage of evolution. And then, lo and behold!, the mighty KGB itself had been obliged by the failed coup [1991] to mutate into two entirely new sets of initials: the SVR – the spies – stationed out at Yusenevo, and the FSB – internal security – still here, in the Lubyanka, with the bones.

Robert Harris, *Archangel*

The collapse of Communism had overwhelmingly positive effects on its former subjects, but in the West we are missing the need to compare ourselves ethically against an ideological antagonist. The welfare state, free universal healthcare, paid holidays, workers' benefits of all kinds – how many of these would we have if it were not for the need to show that the West could not just outcompete Communism, but was ethically superior to it? How much have our rights in these areas grown since Communism collapsed? We're a lot richer, of course. Is that all we now have to say for ourselves? Put it like this: would Guantánamo have happened during the Cold War?

John Lanchester, *London Review of Books*, 2006

Corrections

At Oxford C. B. Fry's party trick was to leap backwards from carpet to mantelpiece from a standing fart.
Guardian, 1972 (first edition)

At Oxford C. B. Fry's party trick was to leap backwards from carpet to mantelpiece from a standing tart.
Guardian, 1972 (second edition)

At Oxford C. B. Fry's party trick was to leap backwards from carpet to mantelpiece from a standing start.
Guardian, 1972 (third edition)

Statements made by Sylvester the Cat were erroneously attributed to Daffy Duck.
Boston Globe, date unknown

An article about decorative cooking incorrectly described a presentation of Muscovy duck by Michel Fitoussi, a New York chef. In preparing it, Mr Fitoussi uses a duck that has been killed.
New York Times, 1981

I realise that the translation of religious documents is open to interpretation, but when I said the Good

Samaritan was 'moved to get off his ass' I feel it translates better using the word 'donkey' rather than your choice of backside.

Letter to the *Newbury Weekly News* by Ron Burke, author of a recent *Christian Viewpoint* article, 1991

In criticizing the political views of Patrick Buchanan, Mr Bennett said: 'It's a real us-and-them kind of thing,' not, as we reported, 'It's a real S and M kind of thing.'

New Yorker, 1995

In our interview with Sir Jack Hayward, the chairman of Wolverhampton Wanderers . . . we mistakenly attributed to him the following comment: 'Our team was the worst in the First Division and I'm sure it will still be the worst in the Premier League.' Sir Jack had just declined the offer of a hot drink. What he actually said was: 'Our tea was the worst in the First Division and I'm sure it will still be the worst in the Premier League.'

Guardian, 2004

In a story in last week's *Express*, it was incorrectly stated that staff who had served five years with Legoland were rewarded with a five-figure sum. It should have stated that they were rewarded with a figure of five, made out of Lego-bricks.

Slough and South Bucks Express, 2004

A story Nov. 15 about mathematical references on 'The Simpsons' TV show mistakenly said that 1,782 to the 12th power plus 1,841 to the 12th power equals 1,922 to the 12th power. Actually, 1,782 to the 12th power plus 1,841 to the 12th power equals

2,541,210,258,614,589,176,288,669,958,142,428,526,657 while 1,922 to the 12th power equals

2,541,210,259,314,801,410,819,278,649,643,651,567,616. Obviously.

San Francisco Chronicle, 2005

[This correction itself had to be corrected, partly because the paper got the date of the original article wrong. The maths might also have been wrong again, too. Shall we move on?]

It was not the author's intention to call New Jersey 'Jew Jersey'.

Denver Daily News, 2005

Norma Adams-Wade's June 15 column called Mary Ann Thompson-Frank a socialist. She is a socialite.

Dallas Morning News, 2005

... The problem arose when the computer spell checker did not recognise the term WNO (Welsh National Opera). A slip of the fingers caused it to be replaced with the word 'winos'.

Liverpool Daily Post, 2005

In our G2 cover story about Hunter S. Thompson we mistakenly attributed to Richard Nixon the view that Thompson represented 'that dark, venal and incurably violent side of the American character'. On the contrary, it was what Thompson said of Nixon.

Guardian, 2005

It has come to our attention that the *Herald-Leader* neglected to cover the civil rights movement. We regret the omission.

Lexington (Kentucky) *Herald-Leader*, 2004

In last week's issue of *Community Life*, a picture caption listed some unusual gourmet dishes that were enjoyed at a Westwood Library party for students enrolled in a tutorial programme for conversational English. Mai Thai Finn is one of the students in the programme and was in the centre of the photo. We incorrectly listed her name as one of the items on the menu.

Community Life (Pascack Valley, New Jersey), 1981

We apologize for the Princess Diana page one headline 'Di goes sex mad' which is still on sale at some locations. It is currently being replaced with a special 72-page tribute issue: 'Farewell to the Princess we all loved. Diana – Her Final Hours.'

Statement by the *National Enquirer* (US) reported by the *Daily Mail*, 1997

Country Life

*'I told them straight,
I wasn't going to have
their rotten old pylon
ruining my view.'*

A kind of healthy grave.
Revd Sydney Smith

All country people hate each other.
William Hazlitt

People don't know about rural England between the last Mystery Autumn Foliage Coach Trip and the Mystery Blossom Journey into Spring. Mud, fog, dripping trees, blackness, floods, mighty rushing winds under doors that don't fit, damp hassocks, sticking organ keys, stone floors and that dreadful smell of decay.

J. L. Carr, *How Steeple Sinderby Wanderers won the FA Cup*

I could have told you the country is the least peaceful and private place to live. The most peaceful and secluded place in the world is a flat in London.

Iris Murdoch, *The Sea, The Sea*

William Dewy, Tranter Reuben, Farmer Ledlow late at
     plough,
Robert's kin and John's and Ned's,
And the Squire, and Lady Susan, lie in Mellstock
     churchyard now!

Thomas Hardy, 'Friends Beyond'

The wind was a torrent of darkness among the
     gusty trees
The moon was a ghostly galleon tossed upon
     cloudy seas
The road was a ribbon of moonlight over the
     purple moor . . .
. . . And there's a tailback between Exits 5 and 6
     westbound on the M4

Graeme Garden, *I'm Sorry I Haven't A Clue*, Radio 4, after Alfred Noyes

From the towns, all Inns have been driven: from the villages most . . . Change your hearts or you will lose your Inns and you will deserve to have lost them. But when you have lost your Inns drown your empty selves, for you will have lost the last of England.
Hilaire Belloc

Shallots, pickling, twelve . . . Onion sets, three . . . Shallots, culinary, twelve . . . Parsnips, three . . . Carrots, three, long . . . Bowl pansies, six blooms . . . Leeks, three . . . Cabbages, two . . . Apples, culinary, six . . . Kidney beans, six pods . . . Peas, six pods . . . Broad beans, six pods.
Horticultural categories at Longtown Show, Herefordshire, 1992, all won by Mr D. Ruck

When you leave your village as a young man you leave it for good. Unless you make a fortune in Australia and then you might return as a sort of false squire, and spend the rest of your life standing everybody drinks and apologizing.
Laurie Lee, quoted in the *Daily Telegraph*, 1994

There are thousands of places like this, thought Peplow, thousands of names on the map – Moreton-in-Marsh, Hinton-in-the-Hedges, Newbottle, Oldborough, Long Buckby, Shortcommon, Great Minden . . . ghastly little settlements. But wonderful places if you happen to live in them. And people hurry back to these places or never leave them; hate other people who live in them, consume their lives organising or tidying them or looting them, become hysterical at the thought of being buried out of them, jockey for the insignificant honours offered by them, look with hostility at the world outside them.

J. L. Carr, *A Day in Summer*

The English have become exiles from their own country. Their relationship with this arcadia is that of some emotional remittance man.

Jeremy Paxman, *The English*

There's more money in bullshit than bulls.

John Perry Barlow, lyricist for The Grateful Dead, on giving up ranching, 1997

Sheep found wondering.

Notice at Newton St Margarets, Herefordshire, c. 1995

Cricket

In 1938 the cartoonist Vicky was wandering down a London street when he saw a newspaper billboard proclaiming 'England in Danger'. 'At last,' thought the Hungarian immigrant, 'at last the stupid complacent English have woken up to the German threat' . . . The English batsmen were struggling, early wickets down cheaply, against the touring Australian cricket side. From that moment, Vicky could never quite take Englishmen seriously, at least as adults.

Dominic Lawson, *Sunday Correspondent*, 1990

He has hit the erogenous zone of the British press by helping Lord's and cricket. You can be an axe-murderer, but if you're an axe-murderer who loves cricket, in Britain you'll be OK.

Lord Gowrie on Sir Paul Getty, *Vanity Fair*, 1994

You do well to love it, for it is more free from anything sordid, anything dishonourable than any game in the world. To play it keenly, honourably, generously, self-sacrificingly is a moral lesson in itself, and the classroom is God's air of sunshine. Foster it, my brothers . . . .

Lord Harris, MCC eminence, *The Times*, 1931

Cricket: slowest game in the world! Fastest game in the world!

Maurice Jules, Guyanese coach in London

Cricket is a game designed by providence for the anal madman.

Attr. A. J. Ayer

It civilizes people and creates good gentlemen. I want everybody to play cricket in Zimbabwe. I want ours to be a nation of gentlemen.

Robert Mugabe, quoted in the *Sunday Times*, 1984

Whereas the Australians hate the Poms, the Poms only despise the Australians.

David Stove, Australian philosopher (d. 1994), explaining why they usually win

> English cricket: Australian stranglehold begins, 273–4; caught between youth and experience, 3; damned in the press, 114, 209, 609; 'dead rubber' syndrome, 472; familiarity through county matches, 103; fear of Australia, 599; lack of self-belief, 496; lack of total commitment, 206–7; local negativity, 609; no fun, 282–3; poor fielding, 49, 636; search for a captain, 609; volatile crowds, 600; weakness against leg-spin, 497.

Index entry to *Out of my Comfort Zone, the Autobiography*, by Steve Waugh (Australian captain 1999–2004)

Where lesser men consulted filth, he read *Wisden*.

Julian Barnes, *Arthur and George* (on Conan Doyle)

CRICKET MATCH

GOOD V EVIL

Lord Baden-Powell (captain)	Adolf Hitler (captain)
Gandhi	Attila the Hun
Albert Schweitzer	Goliath
St Paul	Long John Silver
St Francis	Goebbels
Matthew	Marquis de Sade
Mark	Bluebeard
Luke	Al Capone
John	Goddess Kali
Florence Nightingale	Stalin
Cliff Richard	Salome
	12th man: Jack the Ripper

Umpires: Doubting Thomas and Pontius Pilate

Peter Cook and Dudley Moore, *Not Only But Also*, 1970

An interesting if not necessarily very useful

Dictionary

Adultescent – Anyone over thirty-five addicted to youth culture.

Albany – Scotland north of the Forth–Clyde valley.

Altweibersommer – German for Indian summer (lit. old maid's summer).

Les années yé-yé – French term for the 1960s.

Artificial artificial intelligence – Work normally performed by computers but farmed out to humans.

Astroturfing – Fake PR campaign designed to look like a grassroots movement.

Benevolence – (example given in China's *Official English Dictionary* 1991: we definitely do not apply the policy of benevolence to reactionaries.)

Benny – (at various times, in various places) An overcoat; a straw hat; a Jew; a homosexual; Benzedrine; a brothel; a Filipino transvestite; an inhabitant of the Falkland Islands.*

* This last usage – derived from the dim character in *Crossroads* – was used disparagingly of the islanders by British troops after the 1982 war until it was banned by their commanders. After that, the islanders were reputedly known as 'stills', because they were still bennies.

Birmingham Navy – Lifeboatmen's term for inexperienced sailors.

Borough English – Admirable system of inheritance whereby the youngest son inherited all his father's land. Disliked by the author's two elder (lawyer) brothers.

Borrowed-pot defence – Named after a case in which the lawyer defending a man charged with damaging a neighbour's pot claimed (a) his client never took the pot (b) it was damaged anyway and (c) it was in perfect condition. (*New Republic*, 1988)

Boulevardpresse – German for popular press.

Bronx attaché-case – Ghetto-blaster.

Campanalismo – 'Church-bellism', Italian parochialism.

Childermas – 28 December, Holy Innocents' Day, commemorating the slaughter of children by Herod.

Cinq à sept – A French affair (from the customary hours of assignation).

Commissioners' churches – Those built after the Battle of Waterloo.

Comstockery – Harsh censorship (US, after Anthony Comstock, founder of the Society for the Suppression of Vice).

Cowpat friendship – Firm on top, slippery underneath (West Africa).

The day the Eagle shits – Pay-day in the US Army.

The day the ghost walks – Pay-day in the theatre.

Dead man's hand – A poker hand of two aces, two eights,

all black, which Wild Bill Hickok was said to be holding
when he was shot in the back.

Dog's bollocks – Believed to be an expression invented by
printers to describe the sign :-

Dog's cock – Printer's term for an exclamation mark.

Drongo – Stupid or inept person (Australian slang from a
slow horse of the 1920s).

Embarazada – Spanish for pregnant.

False friends – Foreign words whose English meaning is
not as obvious as they seem, e.g. *embarazada*.

Five-dog night – A very cold one. (Aborigines used captive
live dingos as blankets.)

Fluffragette – Woman with pre-feminist role models.

Freedom fries – French fries, as renamed in the US in
2003. *See also* LIBERTY CABBAGE.

Furry Boots City – Aberdeen (from the local accent, 'Furry
boots are you from?').

Fußballweltmeisterschaftsqualifikationsspiel – German for
World Cup football qualifying match.

Gendarme – Isolated rock pinnacle.

Great Stink – The summer of 1858, when the combination
of a hot summer and a polluted Thames forced
politicians to improve London's sewers.

Great Vowel Shift – English linguistic change, starting
c. 1400, in which e.g. coo, boats and fate became cow,
boots and feet.

Guernsey – An Australian jersey.

Hak a chainik – 'Beat a kettle' in Yiddish. Chatter.

Halcyon – Kingfisher.

Halifax gibbet – A Yorkshire precursor of the guillotine.

Heckle – To comb out flax or hemp fibres.

Ill (or Evil) May Day – 1 May 1517, when the London apprentices rioted against foreigners.

Les immortels – The forty members of the Académie française.

Ir a vendimiar y llevar uvas de postre – Spanish for 'going grape picking and taking grapes for dessert', i.e. taking coals to Newcastle.

Jeu à treize – The name the authorities insisted was used for rugby league in France for about forty years after the war (when it was banned by the Vichy government because of its association with socialism).

Judgement of Paris – The 1976 wine-tasting when a group of French experts unanimously declared Californian wine superior to French in a blind test.

Katyusha – 'Little Katya' – the most popular Russian song of World War Two; the eponymous rocket was thought to sound like the tune's crescendo.

Kent miles – Notoriously slow in bygone times, because of bad roads and heavy clay (slow in recent times too, because of bad trains).

Ladies from Hell – Kilted Scottish regiments.

Liberty cabbage – Sauerkraut, as renamed in the US, 1917.

Lodge – A crop beaten down by wind or rain.

Lushbournes or **Lushburgs** – Fake silver pennies in reign of Edward III, imported from Luxembourg.

McLurg's Law – In news bulletins, 1,000 dead Africans = 50 Frenchmen = 1 Briton (approx). (Named after a BBC news editor.)

McNab – Scottish term for claiming a salmon, a brace of grouse (some say one) and a stag on the same day.

Menefregismo – Italian national inertia (lit. I couldn't give a fuck).

Mono no aware – The sad sensitivity to nature, the appreciation of the world's transience, that is central to Japanese aesthetics.

Moron – Welsh for carrots.

Mountain oysters – New Zealand sheep's testicles fried in breadcrumbs. *See also* ROCKY MOUNTAIN *oysters*.

Nest egg – Natural or artificial egg put down to encourage a hen to lay there.

Pathetic fallacy – The attribution of human emotions or characteristics to inanimate objects or to nature, e.g. *angry clouds*; *a cruel wind*.

Peach-coloured case – Chinese *crime passionel*.

Penang Lawyer – Prickly walking stick used to settle disputes.

Plague of Cadwaladr's Time – AD 664.

Poisson d'avril – French April Fool.

Pons Asinorum – 'Bridge of asses'. Fifth proposition of the first book of Euclid; anything found difficult by beginners.

Prematurely anti-fascist – McCarthyite term for those alleged to be Communists in the 1930s.

Pure (noun) – Dog shit.

Pure-finders – People who collected dog shit in the eighteenth century to sell to tanneries for use in bookbinding.

Rasputitsa – The muddy spring and autumn seasons in western Russia.

Rig – A horse with an undescended testicle.

Rocky Mountain oysters – Buffalo testicles.

Roger Mooretis – Stiff acting.

Rush minute – Equivalent of rush hour in Iowa City, Iowa.

Lo Scroccone – The scrounger – alleged Italian nickname for Tony Blair, freebie-holiday addict.

Seven men of Moidart – Bonnie Prince Charlie's companions at the start of the 1745 Rebellion.

Skyclad Jains – Indian ascetics who walk naked because they are allowed no possessions.

Steeleye Span – A fighting waggoner in a Lincolnshire folk song, adopted by the folk group, 1969.

Terrier – Register or survey of land.

Thankful village – A village where all the men who went away to the First World War survived: there were thirty-one in England, seven of them in Somerset.

Three-inch golden lilies – The bound feet that were regarded as the epitome of Chinese beauty.

Tiswas – Metal device with three or four spikes, one always pointing upwards to deter cavalry (c. 1842).

Tom Pudding – Coal barge (Yorkshire).

Tontine – Financial scheme in which the last surviving member acquires the pot.

Trip to Blanket Cove – Afternoon in bed (forces in the Falklands).

Tripe gumbo – Lancashire Cajun music.

Umami – The 'fifth taste', identified by Japanese scientists: savoury (as opposed to salty, sweet, bitter or sour) and supposedly triggered by monosodium glutamate.

Verlan – French back-slang in which the syllables of words are reversed (e.g. *verlan* = *l'envers*).

Waschlappen – German dishcloths, hence wet people or sissies.

Whispering of the Stars – The tinkling noise made when breath freezes into crystals and falls to the ground at extremely low temperatures in Siberia.

Year Without A Summer – 1816 (caused by the eruption of Mount Tambora, east of Java).

Zyxt – Indicative present, second person, of the verb to see in Kentish dialect. (The last word in the *Oxford English Dictionary*, second edition.)

Drinking

'Not for me, thank you – it keeps me awake all afternoon.'

The general practice of the Persians is to . . . deliberate upon affairs of weight when they are drunk; and then on the morrow, when they are sober, the decision to which they came the night before is put before them by the master of the house in which it was made; and if it is then approved of, they act on it; if not, they set it aside. Sometimes, however, they are sober at their first deliberation, but in this case they always reconsider the matter under the influence of wine.

Herodotus, *The History, Book I*

Sir Robert Walpole once returned 552 dozen empty wine bottles to a single supplier.

***Listener*, 1989**

You mustn't blame en . . . the man's not hisself now; he's in a morning frame of mind. When he's had a gallon of cider or ale, or a pint or two of mead, the man's well enough, and his manners are as good as anybody's in the kingdom.

Thomas Hardy, *Under the Greenwood Tree*

And malt does more than Milton can
To justify God's ways to man.

A. E. Housman, 'Terence, this is stupid stuff'

Champagne: best drop of lager money can buy.

Harry Enfield

In the nineteenth century, America was often jokingly referred to as the 'Alcoholic Republic'. Last century, of the seven native-born Americans awarded the Nobel Prize in literature, five – Sinclair Lewis, Eugene O'Neill, Faulkner, Hemingway and Steinbeck – were alcoholic.

Gordon Burn, *Guardian*, 2005

I think a man ought to get drunk at least twice a year
on principle, so he won't let himself get snotty about it.
Raymond Chandler

Oh, food! During Prohibition, people lived on that,
sometimes for days at a time.
Film: *Cutter's Way* (1981)

On the freezing night of January 16, 1920, with
Prohibition to start at midnight at New York, there
were 10,343 licensed premises in the city. About a month
later there were more than 15,000 speakeasies, and
the number rose every day.
Jimmy Breslin, *Damon Runyon: A Life*

It's the kind of wine he would have drunk if he'd liked the
stuff.
**Colonel Tom Parker, Elvis Presley's manager, on Always Elvis
white wine**

Education

It always surprises me that the proponents of various causes – peace studies, political correctness or family values – should be so anxious that these ideas should be preached to schoolchildren. My experience is that any idea recommended by schoolteachers sends the pupils scurrying off in the opposite direction.

John Mortimer, *Murderers and Other Friends*

There is a widespread notion that children are open, that the truth about their inner selves just seeps out of them. That's all wrong. No one is more covert than a child, and no one has greater cause to be that way. It's a response to a world that's always using a tin-opener on them to see what they have inside, just in case it ought to be replaced with a more useful type of tinned foodstuff.

Peter Høeg, *Miss Smilla's Feeling for Snow*

I was immediately struck by the change that had taken place in his [the Revd Aubrey Upjohn's] appearance since those get-togethers in his study at Malvern House, Bramley-on-Sea, when with a sinking heart I had watched him reach for the whangee and start limbering up the shoulder muscles with a few trial swings. At that period of our acquaintance he had been an upstanding old gentleman about eight feet six in height with burning eyes, foam-flecked lips and flame coming out of both nostrils. He had now shrunk to a modest five foot seven or thereabouts, and I could have felled him with a single blow.

P. G. Wodehouse, *Jeeves in the Offing*

The champion flogger was the Revd Dr John Keate, appointed headmaster of Eton in 1809, who beat an average of ten boys a day (excluding his day of rest on Sundays). On 30 June 1832 came his greatest achievement, the thrashing of over eighty of his pupils. At the end of this marathon, the boys stood and cheered him.

Jeremy Paxman, *The English*

We prepare them for death.

Attr. Dom Wilfrid Passmore, Headmaster of Downside, on the school's purpose, c. 1950

The attributes of a successful university . . . Sex for the students, parking for the faculty, football for the alumni.

Clark Kerr, President of the University of California

'You split an infinitive on *The Nine O'Clock News*.'
'I was under fire at the time.'

Exchange between John Simpson of the BBC and his former Cambridge supervisor, *Cam* magazine, 2001

Fame

Fame is like a river, that beareth up things light and swollen and drowns things weighty and solid.

Francis Bacon

I quickly discovered that the more famous a person is, the less he usually has to say that is interesting, because he has become something of a gramophone record on the subject of himself.

Theodore Zeldin

Man in first-class railway carriage c. 1925, studying the man opposite intently: 'You're Baldwin, aren't you? Weren't you at Harrow in '82? What are you doing now?'

Anecdote

At first, before the Attlees moved into Downing Street, he carried on taking the train home to Stanmore, travelling by himself, a detective following discreetly a few paces behind just in case. Generally he went unrecognized. He had to change at Baker Street, where a woman once approached him, and said: 'Have you ever been told you look just like Mr Attlee?' 'Frequently,' he replied and boarded his train.

Francis Beckett, *Clem Attlee*

I played the tour in 1967 and told jokes and nobody laughed. Then I won the Open next year, told some jokes and everybody laughed like hell.

Lee Trevino, golfer

Sir Elton has a number of rivals in the prima donna stakes – notably Diana Ross, Mariah Carey and Jennifer Lopez. Miss Ross once declared: 'If someone has a big dressing room, I have to have a bigger one.' More recently, Miss Lopez is rumoured to have requested Evian water in which to bathe. And Miss Carey this year demanded that her 3 a.m. arrival at a London hotel was celebrated with a red carpet. But Sir Elton remains in a class of his own. He admits to calling a hotel reception desk to ask the concierge to 'turn the wind down' on a breezy night. In the documentary *Tantrums and Tiaras* – made about him by his partner David Furnish – Sir Elton was shown storming off a tennis court after a woman called 'Yoo-hoo' to him.

Daily Mail, 2005

'I could die in the middle of this interview,' he says hopefully. 'At least I wouldn't have to go to the next one.'

John Updike to the *Washington Post*, 1998

We now have cultural machines so powerful that one singer can reach everybody in the world, and make all the other singers feel inferior because they're not like him.

Once that gets started, he gets backed by so much cash that he becomes a monstrous invader from outer space, crushing the life out of all the other human possibilities. My life has been devoted to opposing that tendency.
Alan Lomax, folk-song collector

Answerphone message in the office of Professor Camille Paglia, American feminist, academic and author (spoken by a man):

You have reached the voicemail line of Professor Camille Paglia. Due to present obligations as a teacher and scholar, Professor Paglia cannot personally return calls. American and Canadian media with official requests for interviews should contact her publishers on . . . International media should contact her agent. Invitations to speak and all other business should be put in writing and sent to Professor Paglia at the Department of Humanities, University of Philadelphia. Do not send faxes. Professor Paglia does not accept them. All packages are opened and inspected by staff. Unsolicited materials without return post may be automatically discarded. Urgent messages outside the above categories may be left on this machine. If you do not receive a letter or reply, please assume Professor Paglia is not interested in your proposal. The Department of Humanities regrets that our current staff does not allow us to respond personally to everyone who writes to Professor Paglia.
Reported in the *Guardian*, 1993

WILLIAM REES-MOGG (former editor of *The Times*): In my
    time I have met two kings, three queens and three
    popes, and I have found none of them remarkable.
RUPERT MURDOCH: Maybe they thought you were a bit of
    a prat too, William.
Exchange reported in the *Spectator*, 1987

Fame has a bloody long sell-by date. It is pumped with
preservatives like long-life milk. But success is like fresh
fruit: it perishes every day.
Luke Goss, singer, quoted in the *Mail on Sunday*, 2001

If I'm such a legend, then why am I so lonely?
Judy Garland

Q: What does 'American Pie' mean?
DON MCLEAN: It means I don't have to work again if I
    don't want to.
Interview

Family Life

'If the police start asking questions I shall just say that you packed your things one night and left me.'

Mom and Pop were just a couple of kids when they got married. He was eighteen, she was sixteen, and I was three.

Start of Billie Holiday's autobiography, *Lady Sings the Blues*

Insanity runs in my family. It practically gallops.

Film: *Arsenic and Old Lace* (1944)

The only truly serious questions are ones that even a child can formulate . . . they are the questions with no answers.

Milan Kundera, *The Unbearable Lightness of Being*

SPEND MORE TIME WITH YOUR KIDS NOW AND I WON'T HAVE TO LATER – SHERIFF MICHAEL F SHEAHAN

Sign at Diversey Station, Chicago, 1998

He was forced to worry once again about nuclear war and the future of the planet. He often had the same secret, guilty thought that had come to him after Ethan was born. From this time on I can never be completely happy. Not that he was before, of course.

Anne Tyler, *The Accidental Tourist*

What is a mother? Someone who puts you to bed when you're wide awake and wakes you up when you're fast asleep.

Ron Moody as Captain Hook in *Peter Pan* at Malvern, Christmas 2005

. . . Motherhood changes you so that you forget you ever had time for small things like despising the colour pink.

Barbara Kingsolver, *Pigs in Heaven*

Children . . . do make you less egotistical. I still manage to think about myself 98 per cent of the time, but at least there is a little window where others can impinge.

Hugh Laurie, quoted in the *Daily Telegraph*, 1998

Playgrounds and parks are empty, thanks to scare stories about abductions . . . about eight children [in the UK] are murdered outside the home each year, compared with about fifty inside.

Priscilla Anderson, Professor of Childhood Studies, London University, quoted in *The Times*, 2003

A year in which my mother died cannot be said to be all bad.

John Osborne

Pavlik Morozov, official hero to generations of Soviet schoolchildren for denouncing his parents as enemies of the state, was himself denounced in Moscow yesterday as an idealised traitor.

Morozov 'is not a symbol of revolution and class consciousness but a symbol of legalised and romanticised treachery', novelist and historian Vladimir Amlinsky wrote in a literary monthly for young people.

For fifty years the boy, murdered in official accounts by rich peasants in revenge for his act, has been presented in Soviet schools as a model of Communist morality and revolutionary devotion.

Portraits of Morozov, aged fourteen when he died in 1932 during Stalin's forced collectivisation of farms, for decades decorated schools and centres for the Young Pioneer organization.

Reuters report, 1988

Food

The meal's first plate bore a chiffonade of lobster and foie gras. Over the next five hours, on a night in November 1975, Craig Claiborne and his companion chewed their way through mounds of caviar, ortolans and truffles, a parfait of sweetbreads, a chaudfroid of woodcock, and a dish of *sots-l'y-laisse* (the 'oysters' extracted from above a chicken's thigh-bone) – to name but a few of the delicacies served at an exceptionally sybaritic 31-course dinner, accompanied by bottles of 1918 Château Latour, 1928 Mouton Rothschild and an 1835 Madeira.

After a suitable time for recovery, Claiborne put pen to paper and wrote an infamous review of the restaurant – Chez Denis, in Paris – for the *New York Times,* of which he was food editor. The piece, entitled 'Just A Quiet Dinner for Two in Paris: 31 Dishes, Nine Wines, a $4000 Check', provoked a cannonade of protest, with more than a thousand enraged letters arriving at the newspaper, including one from the Vatican that described the dinner as 'scandalous'. It did not help that Claiborne remarked after the meal that 'he didn't really feel that stuffed', and that he wrote that 'the presentation of the dishes, particularly the cold dishes, such as the sweetbread parfait and the quail mousse tart, was mundane'.

Obituary, *The Times*, 2000

The point of rubbing garlic on bread is that the taste lingers and gives one the illusion of having fed recently.
George Orwell, *Down and Out in Paris and London*

In Canton . . . the menu listed snake stuffed with shrimps, cobra biscuits, snake and cat soup. The party beside me had ordered serpent-gall liqueur. A posse of waiters arrived with a circular basket from which they pulled out several three-foot snakes. An expert foot was placed on the head and tail of each, and their gall-bladders slit open. From each incision a hard black pellet of bile was plucked out, then the snakes thrown back live into the basket to grow new gall. At the table, meanwhile, the party chatted amiably together. Then the bitter nuggets were dissolved in phials of distilled rice wine, eager hands grasped them, and they were downed in a riot of toasting.

In Cantonese cooking, nothing edible is sacred. It reflects an old Chinese mercilessness towards their surroundings. Every part of every animal – pig stomach, lynx breast, whole bamboo rats and salamanders – is consumed. No Hindu cows or Muslim pigs escape into immunity by taboo. It is the cuisine of the very poor, driven to tortuous invention . . .

In the rowdy, proletarian Wild Game Restaurant, I interrogated the waitress for anything I could bear to eat. But she incanted remorselessly from the menu: Steamed Cat, Braised Guinea Pig (whole) with Mashed Shrimps,

Grainy Dog Meat with Chilli and Scallion in Soya Sauce, Shredded Cat Thick Soup, Fried Grainy Mud-Puppy ('It's a fish,' she said) with Olive Kernels, Braised Python with Mushrooms . . . If I wanted the Steamed Mountain Turtle, she said, I'd have to wait an hour. And Bear's Paws, she regretted, were off.

Colin Thubron, *Behind the Wall*

Do not believe the waiter when he offers you the choice of your dish grilled or fried. In a busy restaurant everything is fried – if the customer has specifically asked for grilled fish, it is fried and then the fat dried off with a few seconds under the grill. Never order cooked oysters in any form . . . Avoid pasta in restaurants other than Italian because it is half-cooked in the morning and then simply plunged into boiling water for a few seconds when someone orders it in the evening. Soup is often kept going for three or four days, simmering away in a bain-marie. Steak so old it is beginning to smell can be revitalised by rubbing it with lemon juice.

Philip Knightley, ex-restaurateur, *A Hack's Progress*

Pap always said, take a chicken when you get a chance, because if you don't want him yourself you can easy find somebody that does, and a good deed ain't never forgot. I never see pap when he didn't want a chicken himself, but that's what he used to say, anyway.

Mark Twain, *Huckleberry Finn*

[About 1950] a Gallup Poll discovered that our idea of a perfect meal was tomato soup, Dover sole, roast chicken, trifle and cheese and biscuits.
Sunday Times, 1999

Although Thomas Jefferson had brought the Parisian recipe for pommes frites to the US in 1802, French fries did not become known until the 1920s . . . [They were] popularised in the United States by World War One veterans who had enjoyed them in Europe and by the drive-in restaurants in the 1930s and 1940s.
Eric Schlosser, *Fast Food Nation*

How are you doing in England? Remember that an elevator's called a lift, a mile's called a kilometre and botulism's called steak and kidney pie.
The Simpsons

Who ordered the poo-poo plate?
Film: *A Bug's Life* (1998)

The Columbian Exchange . . . From the New World, Columbus and his successors brought chocolate, maize, potatoes, French beans, pumpkins, tomatoes, chillies and peppers, pineapples, avocados, paw-paws, peanuts and the turkey and delivered in return wheat, olives, grapes, citrus fruits, bananas, sugar cane, lettuce and cabbage, coffee, rice, cattle, pigs, sheep and horses.
Tom Jaine, *Guardian*, 2005

In America, where sugar is very cheap, a prodigious quantity of it is used in all sorts of ways.

William Cobbett

On his deathbed he [George IV] ordered two pigeons, three steaks, a bottle of wine, a glass of champagne, two glasses of port and a glass of brandy.

Chloe Diski, *Observer*, 2003

We didn't starve but nobody ate chicken unless we were sick or the chicken was.

Bernard Malamud, *Idiots First*

In Paris after the war they had a headline in *Combat* – a left-wing newspaper – which said '*Vive la pamplemousse!*' The grapefruit had returned. In England, meanwhile, there was only one place in the whole country you could buy garlic; an importer called Lucullus in Maiden Lane which sold these little shrivelled-up cloves.

Robert Carrier, *Daily Telegraph*, 1994

If ever stranded in England . . . your object must be money, for you cannot expect to get meat, cake and custard pudding in a land where even the rich live poorer, with regards to diet, than the labouring classes of this country [the US].

W. H. Davies, *Autobiography of a Supertramp*

I've only met one chap in all my life who didn't like peas. And, do you know, he was crackers.
Fred Streeter, gardener

Some vegetables I am fond of. Peas I am relatively neutral about.
Attr. John Major

If a vegetarian eats vegetables, what does a humanitarian eat?
Josh White Jr.

I seemed to have missed *Forever Summer with Nigella* (Channel 4) the way you miss a bride's bouquet. The consequences of catching it are too dire. What a mistaka I mika as Captain Bertorelli used to say. Nigella entered, apparently from a bedroom, trailing a pashmina and saying, 'I have nothing against pleasurable eclecticism.' The hourglass silhouette alone made you blink.

She has a mastery of the double entendre unmatched since Marie Lloyd was ordered not to sing 'She sits among the cabbages and peas' and changed it to 'She sits among the cabbages and leeks'. She punctuates proceedings with a soft gasp. 'U.m.m.' Fish sauce, a substance from which all right-minded people will recoil, is 'wonderfully deep and throatily saline'. When boiling rice 'A bit of stickiness is divine'. She flourished a terrifyingly tumescent vegetable purring, 'I love a juicy, red, fat chilli.' I had a serious fear that it was all in my mind. No, it wasn't. When I see a blackberry, I do not think it is winking at me. A trifle does not remind me of white blankets and soft duvets.

Here is Nigella barbecuing a steak, a very basic procedure for which very basic English usually suffices. 'Black and blue, the way I like my steak cooked. Charred on the outside and quiveringly raw within. I love this and I love the way the barbecue really burns meat so you get a deep . . . salty . . . flavoursome crust. U.m.m. I feel the cavewoman swelling up inside me.' She shot a sideways smile at the camera, whose firmness under fire would have been mentioned in despatches at Rorke's Drift.

Nancy Banks-Smith, *Guardian,* **2002**

A census-taker once tried to test me. I ate his liver with fava beans and a nice Chianti.

Film: *The Silence of the Lambs* **(1991)**

An American Breatharian guru, Wiley Brooks, who claimed not to have eaten for nineteen years, was discredited in the 1980s after he was spotted emerging from a fast-food shop clutching a chicken pie.

Independent, **1999**

Vince Misco of La Casa Gelato, Vancouver, serves 380 different kinds of ice cream including pear with blue cheese and Gorgonzola, curry, liquorice and roasted garlic.

National Post, **1999**

I do not overeat because my mother slapped me when I was five. I overeat because I'm a damned hog.
Dolly Parton, quoted in the *Independent on Sunday*, 1995

Sales of PILCHARDS increased tenfold after being renamed Cornish sardines . . . Merchant navy slang: FRIED EGG ON FRIED BREAD – chicken on a raft (or golf ball on fragmentation bomb); HERRING IN TOMATO SAUCE – HITS; TINNED TOMATOES – train smash; HALIBUT – yellow peril . . . The DURIAN, considered a delicacy in many South-East-Asian countries, is a fruit that smells so foul it is banned from many public places. It is said to taste of sweet vanilla and cooked onions . . . A RAISIN dropped in a glass of champagne will rise and fall indefinitely . . . In Tudor times it was customary to have a SURPRISE PIE, the surprise being that live animals jumped out when it was opened . . . Post-war food rationing continued longer in Britain than anywhere else in Western Europe and MEAT was rationed until July 1954 . . . By 2001, 8.6 billion CHICKENS a year (almost 300 per second) were being slaughtered for food in the US . . . The recipe for an egg-mayonnaise sandwich 'handmade just for you', made by Food Partners of London W3 in 2006, stretched to 127 words and eleven separate E-numbers.

Foreigners

We are, we always have been, and I trust we always shall
be, detested in France.
Duke of Wellington

Pride in self, elegance, sense of theatre, conversation
directed by reason, respect for body as for mind,
reserve, urban use of light and shade, trees in streets,
an environment created to human requirements,
the discretion of love.
**John Colvin, British diplomat, on what he had learned from the
French, *Daily Telegraph* obituary, 2003**

On being asked if he liked the French, he paused, then
said: 'No, I don't think I can say that.'
**Douglas Johnson, Professor of French history, *Daily Telegraph* obituary,
2005**

If you open that Pandora's Box you never know what
Trojan 'orses will jump out.
**Attr. Ernest Bevin, British Foreign Secretary, rejecting the Council of
Europe, c. 1950**

Back in the early seventies, when the French President
Georges Pompidou first took to speaking airily of a

'European Union', Foreign Minister Michel Jobert once asked his colleague Edouard Balladur what exactly it meant. 'Nothing,' replied Balladur. 'But then that's the beauty of it.'

Tony Judt, *Post-War*

I have one simple principle in foreign affairs. I look at what the Americans are doing and then do the opposite. That way I can be sure I'm right.

President Chirac, quoted in the *Daily Telegraph*, 2006

'What you think is realism, cynicism, sarcasm and
    orgasm.'
'In France I could run on that slogan and win.'

Woody Allen, Film: *Deconstructing Harry* (1997)

If you want to interest the French in sport, tell them it's war, and if you want to interest the British in war, tell them it's sport.

Attr. Jean-Pierre Rives, rugby player

A bizarre book claiming that the plane that ploughed into the Pentagon on September 11 never existed, and that the US establishment itself was at the heart of the New York and Washington attacks, has shot to the top of the French bestseller lists to indignation on both sides of the Atlantic.

L'Effroyable Imposture ('The Frightening Fraud'), by Thierry Meyssan, sold out its original run of 20,000 copies within two hours of going on sale. 'We've sold 2,500 copies in 10 days, when a blockbuster novel sells maybe 1,500 in a month,' a spokesman at FNAC Les Halles, one of France's biggest bookshops, said. 'It's a phenomenon.'

Mr Meyssan's conspiracy theory argues that American Airlines flight 77, which killed 189 people when it smashed into the headquarters of the US Defense Department, did not exist, and that the whole disaster was a dastardly plot dreamed up and implemented by the US government.

Guardian, 2002

The great Gaels of Ireland
Are the men that God made mad
For all their wars are merry
And all their songs are sad.

G. K. Chesterton, *The Ballad of the White Horse*

I have reason to believe that the fowlpest outbreaks are the work of the IRA.

Revd Ian Paisley, 1985

Whereas the Irish Nationalists have been wrong about most things, the Irish Unionists have been wrong about everything.

Hubert Butler, quoted in the *Independent on Sunday*, 1992

Ireland . . . a country bursting with genius but with absolutely no talent.
Hugh Leonard, *Observer*, 1985

The Irish problem: that attending upon a quick-witted race being governed by a slow-witted one.
Anon.

They say it's not so bad as they say it is.
Rural postmistress on the Ulster situation, 1996

The Germans . . . people who wouldn't storm a railway station unless they bought a platform ticket first.
Attr. Karl Marx

In the first six months of 2005, the Russian population fell by half a million; by the middle of this century, Russia could lose up to half its people, according to Russian government statistics; life expectancy for men is 56; ten years ago it was 63; every other newborn baby is diagnosed with a disease at birth; there are more abortions every year than babies are born; a quarter of the population lives below the poverty line; Moscow has more billionaires than any other city in the world.
***Death of a Nation*, Channel 4, 2006**

The latest sign of Russia's wealth explosion, the 5,000 rouble (£100) banknote, is to be unveiled by the central bank today. The new note will sit comfortably in the wallets of the country's 88,000 dollar millionaires and 33 billionaires, but is likely to be less useful for most of the population, for whom two of the notes are roughly a month's salary.

Guardian, 2006

An estimated 70 per cent of Japanese parents hire private detectives to ensure prospective in-laws are not Korean.

Guardian, 1979

Although he was second cousin to Emperor Hirohito, Mr Yoshida was known to all his acquaintances as Paddy Murphy.

The death of local resident Kanso Yoshida, reported in the *Liverpool Echo*, 1984

Google lifted the veil this week on one of its best-kept secrets: which nations search for what . . . Pakistanis lead the rankings for 'sex' – with their neighbour and nuclear rival India seldom far behind . . . even though homosexuality is punishable by death in Saudi Arabia, the kingdom ranks No. 2 for searches for 'gay sex', behind the Philippines. And consider the list of cities that most frequently look up *'amour'*, the French word for love. Paris, allegedly a romantic haven, is absent from the top ten. The top three berths went to Rabat, Algiers and Tunis.

International Herald Tribune, 2006

Country where jokes about stupidity are told	Subjects of the jokes
Britain	Irish
United States	Poland (and locally other groups)
Canada (Ontario)	Newfoundlanders (Newfies)
Canada (West)	Ukrainians
Australia	Irish, Tasmanians
New Zealand (North Is.)	Irish, Maoris
New Zealand (South Is.)	Irish, West Coasters
Ireland	Kerrymen
South Africa	Afrikaners (Van der Merwe)
France	Belgians, Swiss (Ouin-Ouin)
Netherlands	Belgians, Limburghers
Germany	Ostfrieslanders
Sweden	Finns, Norwegians
Italy	Southerners
Switzerland	Fribourgers
Greece	Pontians (Black Sea Greeks)
Austria	Carinthians, Burgenlanders
Russia	Ukrainians
Iran	Rashtis (Azerbaijanis from Rasht)
Iraq	Kurds
Israel	Kurdish Jews
Egypt	Nubians
India	Sikhs (Sardarji jokes)
Brazil	Portuguese

Research by Christie Davis, Professor of Sociology at Reading University, reported in the *Daily Telegraph*, 1987

Barely an eighth of the population of FRANCE could speak standard French fluently in 1789 and the figure was probably still less than half in 1914 ... French properties are still sold 'by the candle' – à la bougie. When two candles have burned out, the last bid is considered accepted ... The last witch-burning in IRELAND was at Cloneen, Co. Tipperary in 1895 ... In 2004 a plaque to Father Pat Noise 'who died under mysterious circumstances when his carriage plunged into the Liffey on August 10, 1919' appeared on O'Connell Bridge in Dublin City Centre – council officials noticed it in 2006. There is no record of any Father Noise ... English visitors were so common in ITALY in the nineteenth century that all foreigners were known as 'Inglesi' ... There are three-quarters of a million people of Japanese descent in BRAZIL ... LIECHTENSTEIN is the world's largest supplier of false teeth ... Huskies are the only dogs permitted north of the Arctic Circle in GREENLAND to preserve the purity of the bloodline ... Until 1993 in Italy civil servants could retire as 'baby pensioners': even a toilet cleaner who began work at eighteen could retire on a 90 per cent pension at thirty-three ... In 1991 BENIN became the first African country where an incumbent leader ran for re-election, lost and graciously bowed out ... A compulsory sterilization programme 'to improve the population' continued in SWEDEN until 1976 ... BOLIVIA has had more than 190 coups d'état since independence in 1825 ... According to the CIA in 2006, ANDORRA has the world's highest life expectancy at birth

(83.51), SWAZILAND the lowest (32.62), the UK was 38th (78.54); BRITAIN, THE US, BURMA AND LIBERIA are reported to be the only countries that in 2006 still had their road signs in miles.

Gambling

Gaming is a disease of barbarians superficially civilized.
Dean Inge

A Smith and Wesson beats four aces.
Anon.

'I do not know anything about boat races,' Sam says, 'and the Yales may figure as you say, but nothing between human beings is one to three. In fact,' Sam the Gonoph says, 'I long ago come to the conclusion that all life is six to five against.'
Damon Runyon, *A Nice Price*

That's what it's all about, making the wrong move at the right time.
Film: *The Cincinnati Kid* (1965)

When he was about fourteen, the parents of Ray Hitchcock [later a professional cricketer] took his bets for a month in an attempt to cure him of gambling. He won £93 and bought a whippet.
Jack Bannister

Rigg's [spokesman for Camelot] self-satisfied smirk is bound to remind some of the army general who was called in to clean up the Philippine lottery which, because of accusations of corruption, had lost the confidence of the people. He cleaned it up all right. Guess who won the very next draw.

Paul Haigh, *Racing Post*, 1994

A lottery is a taxation
Upon all the fools in creation
And heaven be praised
It is easily raised;
Credulity's always in fashion.

Henry Fielding, play: *The Lottery* (1731)

Screaming Lord Sutch has put £5 on himself to be the next Prime Minister at 15 million to one, which is even longer odds than the 14 million to one we're offering against Elvis Presley crash-landing a UFO on the head of the Loch Ness monster. A man from West London put £1 on that last summer. He said: 'You never know.'

Graham Sharpe, spokesman for William Hill, *The Times*, 1997

I wish that figure was the correct one. The reality is much worse.

Businessman Sir Hugh Fraser on reports that he had gambled away one and a half million pounds, 1981

Jones brought to the game his own special quality. He noticed first, he told me later, in what part of the hand an inexperienced opponent kept his discards and by that means judged how near he was to a gin. He knew by the way his opponent arranged his cards, by the length of his hesitation before playing, whether they were good, bad or indifferent, and if the hand were obviously good he would often propose fresh cards in the certainty of refusal. That gave his opponent a sense of superiority and of security, so that he would be inclined to take risks, to play on too long in the hope of a grand gin. Even the speed with which his opponent took a card and threw one down told him much. 'Psychology will always beat mere mathematics,' he said to me once, and it was certain that he beat me nearly always.

Graham Greene, *The Comedians*

VIVIAN [POOLS WINNER]: We spend hundreds of pounds at the Miners Arms on all our old mates. But they're not mates any more, really. Not now. They've nowt to talk to us about. So they don't. *No* one does. It's like everyone's a stranger. Or *we* are.

Jack Rosenthal, TV play: *Spend, Spend, Spend*, 1977

Bishops see nothing incongruous or outrageous in officiating with their blessings at the launching of Polaris submarines; but they have never been known to open casinos or race tracks. For their propensity to swallow unethical camels and strain at imaginary moral gnats, the Christian churches are unsurpassed.

Phil Bull, founder of *Timeform*, 1989

Headlines

SIXTY HORSES WEDGED IN CHIMNEY
(The story to fit this sensational headline has not yet
turned up)
'Beachcomber', *Daily Express*

TITANIC GOES DOWN. EVERYONE SAFE.
Daily Mirror, 1912

BOTH SIDES AGREE NOT TO BOMB CIVILIANS
Washington Post, 3 September 1939

CRY OF 'FILTHY BEAST' IN THE CINEMA
Attr. *News of the World*, c. 1955

NUDIST WELFARE MAN'S MODEL WIFE
FELL FOR THE CHINESE HYPNOTIST
FROM THE CO-OP BACON FACTORY
News of the World, c. 1965

SEX-CHANGE NUN IS NOW TV WRESTLER
National Examiner, 1986

I UPPED MY INCOME. UP YOURS.
Attr. *Reader's Digest*

MAN BUYS WORLD
Business Week, on Rupert Murdoch, 1995

BANFF WAS DEAD COMEDIAN'S FAVOURITE HOLIDAY RESORT
Attr. *Aberdeen Press and Journal*, 1977, on the death of Charlie Chaplin

IRAQI THREAT TO PETERSFIELD BY-PASS
Petersfield Post, 1990

MEN AND WOMEN: WE ARE STILL DIFFERENT
USA Today, 1988

WHY THE NEW CINEMA IN THE PHILIPPINES ISN'T VERY INTERESTING
Attr. *Le Monde*

THE WORST DISASTER IN THE HISTORY OF THE WORLD, page 8
Evening Standard, on the Bangladesh floods of 1970

UNIONS GEAR UP TO DEFEND SCHOOLING
Morning Star, 12 September 2001, page 1

TERRORISTS DESTROY WORLD TRADE CENTRE
Morning Star, 12 September 2001, page 2

Jews

Anti-Semitism: the socialism of fools.
August Bebel

The many generations who have no doubt admired
them since can rarely have thought of the stricken Jews
walking, throughout October 1290 [after being expelled
by Edward I], towards the harbours of Kent and London
before the 1 November deadline for their departure
(All Saints' Day). One of the boats commissioned to
carry them away struck a sandbar in the Thames estuary.
The captain invited his passengers to disembark and
stretch their legs, then sailed gleefully off the mudflat,
shouting to the bereft refugees that they should seek
help from Moses. Maybe they tried. But no one came to
their aid. The sea did not part. They all drowned.
Robert Winder, *Bloody Foreigners*

Almost poetically symptomatic of the Jews' terminal
condition was the practice of teachers at Jewish
kindergartens in Berlin during the early part of the war
of letting their charges spend their playtime among
tombstones: the communal cemetery was the only patch
of green from which wearers of the Yellow Star were not
debarred. A typical scene took place at a Berlin

greengrocer's, when a four-year-old Jewish girl begged her mother for some cherries; when told the fruit was excluded from the Jewish ration she ran out of the shop crying. Since no one else was about it would have been quite easy for the shopkeeper to make the child happy, instead of which he observed the incident with imperturbable indifference. Shopkeepers did not always honour even the already meagre Jewish ration cards, identifying denial of food to Jews with their patriotic duty. Women shopkeepers tended to be worse than men.
Richard Grunberger, *A Social History of the Third Reich*

So thoroughly did they [Jewish Hollywood moguls] reject their pasts that when Danny Kaye was brought to Hollywood, Sam Goldwyn ordered his hair dyed blond, in order to downplay what other Hollywood Jews called Kaye's 'sinister' or too Jewish look.
***New York Review of Books*, 1989**

In his memoir, *Eichmann in My Hands* (1990), Mr. Malkin described being surprised at how undistinguished and rather bony Eichmann looked. He was expecting a 'monster'. He said his interrogations were freakishly revealing, as when he confronted Eichmann about the death of Mr. Malkin's nephew in Poland: 'My sister's boy, my favourite playmate, he was just your son's age. Also blond and blue-eyed, just like your son. And you killed him.' Mr. Malkin wrote: 'Genuinely perplexed by the observation, he actually waited a moment to see if I would clarify it. "Yes," he said finally, "but he was Jewish, wasn't he?" '

Obituary of Peter 'Zvika' Malkin, Adolf Eichmann's captor, *Washington Post*, 2005

In the honour roll of countries who resisted the Nazi effort to exterminate the Jewish people, Denmark, Finland and Bulgaria are remembered as defiant beacons of light . . . Albania's achievement in saving all its Jews is even more remarkable when contrasted with the fate of Jews in neighbouring Greece, where 90 per cent of the Jewish community perished . . . Albanian underground fighters issued an order in 1943 that anyone refusing to give refuge to those in need would be subject to execution 'for the crime of disgracing the Albanian people'. It is believed no one betrayed this order.

Jack Goldfarb, frosina.org, 1999

I wasn't afraid of the Germans. I was afraid of the Poles.

Rosemarie Kupferman, survivor of the Warsaw Ghetto

The main target of [post-war] popular vengeance was frequently Jews . . . in the eighteen months following the end of World War Two, more Jews were killed in Poland, Hungary and Czechoslovakia than in the ten years preceding the war . . . 150 Jews were killed in liberated Poland in the first four months of 1945. By April 1946 the figure was nearly 1,200 . . . in the fourth *arrondissement* of Paris on April 19, 1945, hundreds of people demonstrated in protest when a returning Jewish deportee tried to redeem his (occupied) apartment . . . the crowd screaming 'La France aux français'.

Tony Judt, *Post-War*

O God of Mercy
For the Time Being
Choose Another People

Kadia Moladowsky, Yiddish poet, c. 1945

I have not made a study of the subject but believe that it is a minor point in the history of the war.

Jean-Marie Le Pen on the Holocaust, *Daily Telegraph*, 1987

It [Palestine 1946] was a country of so-what people. So what you are cold and hungry? Let me tell you where *I* have been. *I* know cold and hunger. So what you miss your mother? *My* mother was gassed. And my father and my grandparents and my sisters and brothers. So what you want your boyfriend? *My* boyfriend was murdered by British soldiers. I was never going to outdo them. They had skins like elephant hides and they brandished their suffering at you like heavy clubs. They'd bash your brains out with those clubs if they could.

Linda Grant, *When I Lived in Modern Times*

Now we have Jewish policemen arresting Jewish
criminals and Jewish prostitutes – our own country.
Attr. Israeli police chief, c. 1948

I don't want my children to get too much religious
training – just enough to know what religion they aren't
observing.
New York Jewish parent, c. 1945

You think in the Diaspora, it's abnormal. Come live here
[in Israel]. This is the homeland for Jewish abnormality.
Worse: now we are the *dependent* Jews, on your money,
your lobby, on our big allowance from Uncle Sam, while
you are the Jews living interesting lives, comfortable
lives without apology, without shame and perfectly
independent . . . The fact remains that in the Diaspora a
Jew like you lives securely, without real fear of
persecution and violence, while we are living just the
kind of imperilled Jewish existence which we came here
to replace . . . We are the excitable, ghettoized, jittery
little Jews of the Diaspora and you are Jews with all the
confidence and cultivation that comes from feeling at
home where you are.
Philip Roth, *The Counterlife*

It is forbidden to be merciful to them [the Arabs].
You must send missiles to them and annihilate them.
They are evil and damnable. May the Holy Name visit

retribution on the heads of the Arabs and cause their seed to be lost.

Rabbi Ovadiah Yossef, founder of the Israeli Shas Party, *Daily Telegraph*, 2001

The world at large may, indeed, have no right whatever to apply a double standard of ethical political action to the Jew. The Jew must apply it to himself.

Attr. George Steiner

I couldn't even contemplate drinking a glass of milk with my salami sandwich without giving serious offence to God Almighty. Imagine then what my conscience gave me for all that jerking off!

Philip Roth, *Portnoy's Complaint*

Wherever we go, we don't adapt to the place or the people . . . it's the place and the people who have to adapt to us.

Orthodox Jew in Iowa, quoted by Stephen G. Bloom, *Postville*

I'm not Jewish any more. I'm Scientific American.

Harvey Fierstein, play: *Torch Song Trilogy* (1982)

Language

*'I'm English – and if I come out of anything
I'll come out of the cupboard.'*

... they indulged their predilection for Shit Patois ...
to mean possessions ('Where's your shit?'), lies or
misleading explanations ('Are you shitting me?', 'We need
a shit detector'), drunk ('shit-faced'), trouble ('in deep
shit'), ineptitude ('couldn't play point guard for shit'), care
about ('give a shit'), rude, thoughtless, disloyal ('really

shitty thing to do'), not kidding ('no shit?'), obnoxiously unpleasant ('he's a real shit'), mindless conversation ('talking shit', 'shooting the shit'), confusing story ('or some such shit'), drugs ('you bring the shit?'), to egest ('take a shit'), to fart in such a way that it becomes partly egestion ('shart'), a trivial matter ('a piece a shit'), unpleasantly surprised ('he about shit a brick'), ignorance ('he don't know shit'), pompous man ('the big shit', 'that shitcake'), hopeless situation ('up Shit Creek'), disappointment ('oh, shit!'), startling ('holy shit!'), unacceptable, inedible ('shit on a shingle'), strategy ('oh, *that* shit again'), feces, literally ('shit'), slum ('some shithook neighborhood'), meaningless ('that don't mean shit'), et cetera ('and messages and shit'), self-important ('he thinks he's *some shit*'), predictably ('sure as shit'), very ('mean as shit'), verbal abuse ('gave me shit'), violence ('before the shit came down' or 'hit the fan', 'don't start no shit', 'won't be no shit'). Still, they didn't neglect Fuck Patois . . .

Tom Wolfe, *I Am Charlotte Simmons*

He's a helluva guy. Wouldn't say shit if he had a mouthful.

Jim Bouton, baseball player

Cliché is the natural language we use to express our strongest emotions.

John Galsworthy

Swift . . . once wrote to the Earl of Oxford to express his outrage that words like bamboozle, uppish and – of all things – couldn't were appearing in print.

Simon Winchester, *The Professor and the Madman*

English travellers and reviewers [with their] pious horror of Americanisms . . . were able, for a while, to shut off their flow into Standard English, but only for a while. The tide began to turn . . . in 1820, and soon thereafter a large number of Yankee neologisms that had been resisted with heroic dudgeon came into common use in England e.g. reliable, influential, talented and lengthy.

H. L. Mencken, *The American Language*

. . . the exoneration of Anglo-Saxon, for so long thought the source and origin of our favourite swear words. It has been suggested that it was English sixteenth-century sailors who brought in 'fokkinge', 'krappe' and buggere' . . . which they found irresistible in Low Dutch. Even when they are found in earlier English, these words are not swear words. Cunt is not taboo.

Melvyn Bragg, *The Adventure of English*

Almost all the hundred most common words in our language worldwide, wherever it is spoken, come from Old English. There are three from old Norse, 'they', 'their' and 'them', and the first French-derived word is 'number', in at seventy-six.

1 the	21 at	41 there	61 some	81 my
2 of	22 be	42 use	62 her	82 than
3 and	23 this	43 an	63 would	83 first
4 a	24 have	44 each	64 make	84 water
5 to	25 from	45 which	65 like	85 been
6 in	26 or	46 she	66 him	86 call
7 is	27 one	47 do	67 into	87 who
8 you	28 had	48 how	68 time	88 oil
9 that	29 by	49 their	69 has	89 its
10 it	30 word	50 if	70 look	90 now
11 he	31 but	51 will	71 two	91 find
12 was	32 not	52 up	72 more	92 long
13 for	33 what	53 other	73 write	93 down
14 on	34 all	54 about	74 go	94 day
15 are	35 were	55 out	75 see	95 did
16 as	36 we	56 many	76 number	96 get
17 with	37 when	57 then	77 no	97 come
18 his	38 your	58 them	78 way	98 made
19 they	39 can	59 these	79 could	99 may
20 I	40 said	60 so	80 people	100 part

Bragg, op. cit.

Ours is not the only language and culture in which
h-dropping among the common people is stigmatized;
we are told that Galilean speakers of Aramaic in New
Testament times were well known for this tendency,
so that Jesus Christ almost certainly dropped his *h*s.
It was thus not inappropriate that a BBC Schools Radio
programme on the life of Christ in September 1985

should have endowed him with a Yorkshire accent, since Yorkshire folk are among those whose accent permits *h*-dropping, as do all the urban accents of England . . . except the Geordie accent of Tyneside.

John Honey, *Does Accent Matter?*

Hindi, you see, is spare and beautiful. In it we can think thoughts that have the merit of simplicity and truth . . . English is not spare. But it is beautiful. It cannot be called truthful because its subtleties are infinite. It is the language of people who have probably earned their reputation for perfidy and hypocrisy because their language itself is so flexible.

Paul Scott, *The Jewel in the Crown*

Last year this newspaper reported the existence, in the Bantu language Tshiluba, of the long-needed word *ilunga*, meaning 'a person who is ready to forgive any abuse for the first time, to tolerate it a second time, but never a third time'. Subsequent investigations suggested that the word may not exist in Tshiluba, but it exists now in English, as thousands of entries on the web attest.

Ben Macintyre, *The Times*, 2006

Kingsley Amis, challenged to produce a sentence whose meaning depended on an apostrophe, came up with: Those things over there are my husbands.

Letter to the *Guardian*, 2006

The Law and the Lawless

'I think the jury has been got at, my lord.'

That you be conveyed from hence to the place from which you came, and from thence you be drawn to the place of execution, upon hurdles; That you be there severally hanged by the neck; That you be cut down alive; That your privy members be cut off; That your bowels be taken out, and burned in your view; That your heads be severed from your bodies; That your bodies be divided into four quarters, and your quarters to be at the king's dispose. And the God of infinite mercy be merciful to your souls.

Sentence passed on Popish plotters, 1679

JUDGE: You are sentenced to be hanged by the neck until you are dead, dead, dead.

BILLY THE KID: And you can go to hell, hell, hell.

Dee Brown, *The American West*

By 1753, when the death penalty was abolished [in Russia] in favour of lifelong labour, the variety of offences punishable by exile had grown bewildering. Prize-fighting, wife-beating, begging with false distress, illicit tree-felling, vagrancy and fortune-telling might all condemn a man to Siberia, as well as the European innovations of taking snuff (exile was accompanied by ripping out the nostrils' septum) or driving a cart with the use of reins.

Colin Thubron, *In Siberia*

As doctors seldom take their own prescriptions, and divines do not always practise what they preach, so lawyers are shy of meddling with the law on their own account, knowing it to be an edged tool of uncertain application, very expensive in the working, and rather remarkable for its properties of close shaving, than for its always shaving the right person.

Charles Dickens, *The Old Curiosity Shop*

The law is like a telegraph pole: hard to climb but easy to get round.

Anon.

Justice and law could be described as very distant cousins and here in South Africa they are not on speaking terms at all.

Film: *A Dry White Season* (1989)

Cross-examination, my father used to say, must never be confused with examining crossly.

John Mortimer, *Murderers and Other Friends*

The murderer should be a little man of the professional class – a dentist or a solicitor, say, living an intensely respectable life somewhere in the suburbs, preferably in a semi-detached house, which will allow the neighbours to hear suspicious sounds through the wall. He should be either chairman of the local Conservative Party branch or a leading Nonconformist and strong Temperance advocate . . . The means chosen should, of course, be poison.

George Orwell, *Decline of the English Murder*

Like a headmaster at a preparatory school: punctilious, refined, vindictive.

Cecil Beaton on the strangler John Christie, 1953

Are you sure this is safe?

William Palmer, the Rugeley poisoner, ascending the scaffold, 1856

In terms of the sub-culture in which I was socialized in the South London streets, it was the norm for disputes between man and man to be settled between man and man.

Gangster Charles Richardson, 1980, after taking a psychology degree in prison

I wouldn't live in London now. You can't walk down the street without being mugged.

Attr. Reggie Kray, gangster, 1983

I only wish Peter had joined the police. He had the qualities to make a good policeman.

Attr. the father of Yorkshire Ripper Peter Sutcliffe, *Sun*, 1981

Norwood Conservative Party calls upon the Government to recreate the conditions in which a virgin leading a child and carrying a bag of gold could pass on foot from one end of the kingdom to another without fear.

Motion at Party Conference, 1982

Injustice is relatively easy to bear. What stings is justice.

H. L. Mencken

I'm about to be tried by 12 people too stupid to get out of doing jury service.

Reported graffito, Old Bailey gents, c. 2000

Junior Allen, sixty-five, was released from jail in NORTH CAROLINA in 2005 after serving thirty-five years for stealing a black-and-white television set . . . Boiling to death became an approved method of capital punishment under Henry VIII ... In seventeenth-century Virginia stealing grapes and killing chickens were capital crimes; in New York Colony striking a parent was; in North Carolina, by the early nineteenth century, it was a capital offence to hide a slave with intent to free him ... The judge in the Jack Ruby murder case in Texas was known as 'Necessity' Brown, because necessity knows no law ... In the UK, Myra Hindley's dog Puppet died under anaesthetic while being X-rayed: 'You're a lot of fucking murderers,' she told the police.

Leaders

In our every deliberation we must consider the impact of our decisions on the next seven generations.

From the Great Law of the Iroquois Confederacy, pre-1500

If the subject is seen to live frugally, tell him because he is clearly a money saver of great ability he can afford to give generously to the King. If, however, the subject lives a life of great extravagance, tell him he, too, can afford to give largely, the proof of his opulence being evident in his expenditure.

John Morton, Chancellor of England, 1487 ('Morton's Fork')

To think what time was wasted in arguing about the House of Lords, Tories saying it ought to be preserved because it was clever, and Radicals saying it ought to be destroyed because it was stupid, and all the time no one saw that it was right because it was stupid, because that chance mob of ordinary men thrown there by accident of blood were a great democratic protest against the Lower House, against the eternal insolence of the aristocracy of talents.

G. K. Chesterton, *The Napoleon of Notting Hill*

The patrician High Tory wing of the party then devoted their energies to opposing votes for women, with Curzon characteristically leading this resistance, and then characteristically surrendering. They did not realize that they had inadvertently stumbled upon the Conservative salvation . . . from the moment they were enfranchised women voted predominantly Conservative.

Geoffrey Wheatcroft, *The Strange Death of Tory England*

It's the god-damnest thing. There was this whippersnapper, malaria-ridden and yellah, sickly, sickly. He never said a word of importance in the Senate and he never did a thing . . . His growing hold on the American people was simply a mystery to me.

Lyndon Johnson on John Kennedy

What's all this Nixon nonsense about? We all bug our opponents, don't we?

Mao Tse-Tung to Edward Heath

When the President does it, it means it's not illegal.

Richard Nixon

The other guys were going crazy because they couldn't get the solution. This guy doesn't even know there's a problem.

Jackie Mason on Ronald Reagan

The Clinton Administration may be the first in the nation's history to have in top policy positions more people who have gone through therapy than through military service.

Michael Kelly, *New Yorker*, 1994

In 1996 Hillary Clinton was asked to identify her husband's character flaws: 'Hogging the remote control and chewing ice,' she said.

Roger Simon, *Showtime*

Nixon, Reagan and Clinton find themselves in Oz. They go to the Emerald City and meet the Wizard, who grants each one a wish. 'I want a brain,' says Reagan. 'I want a heart,' says Nixon. 'That young lady and her dog still around?' says Clinton.

Joke, c. 1998

The historian A. N. Wilson recounted last week the experience of an eighteen-year-old girl who told her mother that Herbert Asquith 'had seized her hand under the dinner table and thrust it into his trousers'. The mother replied that, since he was Prime Minister, he could do as he liked. 'At least he was better than Lord Kitchener,' she added.

***Independent on Sunday*, 1997**

If you own up in a genial sort of way, the House of Commons will forgive you anything.

Hugh Whitemore, play: *A Letter of Resignation* (1997)

I like the House of Commons. It's the only place where I can express my views without the slightest chance that they'll leak out to a wider audience.

Kenneth Clarke

If Mr Norman Fowler, for example, merely delivers something like the Gettysburg Address when winding up the evening debate, there will not be a line of it in the papers next morning: whereas if a minister's teenage daughter is unlucky enough to be found at midnight *in flagrante delicto* in a squat in Catford, the *Sun* will clear its front page.

Julian Critchley, *Palace of Varieties*

I dined with Victor Cazalet at the House of Commons. After dinner I went up to the Strangers' Gallery. I felt how easy it would be to dominate the mediocrities there, but what would be the use? . . . If anybody spoke as badly as that at the Peckham debating club they would be howled down.

Beverley Nichols

Harry Tate [the music-hall artist] was once taken along to the House of Commons by Wee Georgie Wood and had to be escorted out. Halfway through the debate Tate gave a great snort of laughter from the public gallery and said loudly, 'They think it's all real, you know.' It's in Hansard – a stranger was escorted from the gallery.

Roy Hudd, *Sunday Times*, 1982

It is said that roosters think the sun rises because they crow. Politicians are much the same.

Charles Murray, US Libertarian

On October 16, 1854, in Peoria, Illinois, Douglas [Lincoln's rival for the Senate] delivered a three-hour address to which Lincoln, by agreement, was to respond. When Lincoln's turn came, he reminded the audience that it was already 5 pm, that he would probably require as much time as Douglas and that Douglas was still scheduled for a rebuttal. He proposed, therefore, that the audience go home, have dinner, and return refreshed for four more hours of talk. The audience amiably agreed . . . Typically, at county or state fairs, programmes included many speakers, most of whom were allotted three hours for their arguments.

Neil Postman, *Amusing Ourselves to Death*

Being an MP feeds your vanity and starves your self-respect.

Matthew Parris, *The Times*, 1994

Congressmen are like diapers: you need to change 'em often, and for the same reason.

Pete McCloskey, ex-Congressman, 2006

After two years in Washington, I missed the sincerity and genuineness of Hollywood.

Fred Thompson, Senator and actor, 1996

If you agree with me on nine out of twelve issues, vote for me. If you agree with me on twelve out of twelve issues, see a psychiatrist.

Ed Koch, running for Mayor of New York, 1989

You are not here to tell me what to do. You are here to tell me why I have done what I have already decided to do.

Attr. Montagu Norman, Governor of the Bank of England, to his economic adviser

Now note the benignity of your prince. Now note how easily ye may have pardon, both gentlemen and other if ye list. Now note how effusion of blood may be eschewed. Now note, what this little while of a rebellion hath hindered yourselves and country. Now learn by a little lack to eschew a worse. Now learn, by this small warning, to keep you true men.

Henry VIII to rebels in Yorkshire, 1537

I am beginning to believe there is nothing so dangerous as cleverness in an administrator. Give me a stupid old country gentleman.

Lord Robert Cecil on Lloyd George

None of you, I insist, must ever say I'm dictatorial again.

Neville Chamberlain to lobby journalists

Rien.

Louis XVI's diary entry, 14 July 1789

Henry [Kissinger] does not lie because it is in his interest. He lies because it is in his nature.

Helmut Sonnenfeld, State Department official, 1975

What is politics? Politics is when you say you are going to do one thing while intending to do another. Then you do neither what you said nor what you intended.

Attr. Saddam Hussein, 1979

They say he read Homer for fun, which serves him right.

Churchill on Gladstone

I never forgive. I always forget.

Arthur Balfour

Many years ago, when he was Prime Minister, Mr Attlee joined a trio of young Tories at the dinner table, of which I was one. 'You know,' he said, 'we sometimes in a friendly way make up a cricket XI here of four-letter fellows. Oddly, it is always pretty evenly divided among the parties.'

W. F. Deedes, *Daily Telegraph*, 1994

'If I lived here, I wouldn't vote for Harold Wilson. And I wouldn't vote for myself either.'
'Who would you vote for?'
'Robespierre.'

Attr. Edward Heath, visiting the Newcastle slums

Not a bad man, just a slob.

Alice Roosevelt Longworth on President Harding

He had no ideas and he was not a nuisance.

H. L. Mencken on President Coolidge

He [President Buchanan, 1857–61] tried to keep the peace. That whole decade of Presidents did, Fillmore, Pierce and Buchanan . . . And precious little thanks they've got from history for it – the doughface Presidents. History loves blood. It loves the great blood-spillers.

John Updike, *Memories of the Ford Administration*

I know a Prime Minister who picks his nose and regales himself with the contents. I solemnly declare this to be true. I have witnessed this worse than beastly act dozens of times.

William Cobbett on Lord Liverpool

David Davis [a Conservative politician] says: 'My principles are 200 years old: low taxation, a small state and help for those in need.' Even then William Hazlitt referred to them as the old conservative remedy, to take nothing from the rich, and give it to the poor.

Letter to the *Guardian* from Harry Jones of Cambridgeshire, 2005

Unfortunately it's impossible. Or very difficult. Or highly inadvisable. Or would require legislation. One of those.

Sir Humphrey Appleby in *Yes Minister*

Under consideration means we've lost the file. Under active consideration means we're trying to find it.
Yes Minister

It is hard to overstate the influence of *Yes Minister* on every generation of politicians since it was first screened a quarter of a century ago. Sir Humphrey has passed into the language, and civil servants, especially senior ones, are perceived as threats to initiative and originality.
Max Hastings, *Guardian*, 2006

You have told me well the interests of HMG. What are the interests of mankind?
Michael Stewart, Foreign Secretary, to official, c. 1968

I never think you can judge any country by its politics. All we English are quite honest by nature.
Film: *The Lady Vanishes* (1938)

His overdraft at Allied Irish Banks in January was more than £1m. In the same month he made a dramatic plea to the nation, broadcast by state television, urging the necessity of fiscal restraint.
Obituary of Charles Haughey, Irish Prime Minister, *Daily Telegraph*, 2006

Hypocrisy is the Vaseline of political intercourse.
Pieter-Dirk Uys

If you have two guys and one's got the solution to the Middle East and the other guy falls in the orchestra pit, who do you think's going to make the evening news and the front pages?

Roger Ailes, President Bush I's media adviser, 1989

The people have spoken, the bastards.

Dick Tuck, Californian politician

Almost anyone can run for President up here [New Hampshire], as long as you meet a couple of minimum entry qualifications and file the $1,000 fee with New Hampshire's Secretary of State. Alas, the best President we never had got kicked out of the race. That was the 1980 Vegetarian Party candidate, Colossus G. Benson from Benson's Wild Animal Farm in Hudson, New Hampshire. He was a 475 lb gorilla, but there's apparently nothing in the constitution to prevent primates running for President. However, the receptionist at the State House in Concord said she wasn't going to let a gorilla wander the corridors looking for the office of Secretary of State William Gardner and she detained him in the lobby. 'So he sent in his campaign manager,' says Mr Gardner, 'a chimpanzee in a white suit.' Unfortunately, the Secretary of State was obliged to point out that the constitution requires a President be at least thirty-five years old, and the gorilla was only twelve. So Mr Gardner gave the chimp back his thousand bucks.

Mark Steyn, *Daily Telegraph*, 1999

BOADICEA is said to be buried under Platform 10 at King's Cross Station ... GENERAL VIDELA of Argentina always wore gloves in public, apparently because he was a nail-biter ... The 8TH DUKE OF DEVONSHIRE (who served in three of Gladstone's ministries) said the proudest moment of his life came when his pig won first prize at Skipton Fair ... Iowa Congressman H. R. GROSS complained, in the midst of national mourning for President Kennedy, about the fuel bill for the eternal flame ... In 1940, LORD HALIFAX's secretary omitted to tell him that R. A. Butler was in his outer office with a message that Labour would serve under him; Halifax slipped out of the other door to go to the dentist, and by evening Churchill was Prime Minister ... OLIVER CROMWELL's original family name was Williams ... ANDREW BONAR LAW and NEVILLE CHAMBERLAIN are the only twentieth-century Prime Ministers buried in Westminster Abbey ... CHAMBERLAIN was named as one of the world's eleven most glamorous people by a US committee in 1938 ... LORD ROSEBERY's cabinet (c. 1894) reputedly once spent a large part of a session discussing the exact text of one of Juvenal's satires ... Australians traditionally sent dead cats as a sign of dislike: the former Labour leader ARTHUR CALWELL claimed to have received thirty after one speech ... GLADSTONE and his wife would sing together

> *'A ragamuffin husband and a rantipoling wife*
> *We'll idle it and scrape it through the ups and downs*
> *   of life.'*

Liberty

It was artfully contrived by Augustus that, in the enjoyment of plenty, the Romans should lose the memory of freedom.

Edward Gibbon, *Decline and Fall of the Roman Empire*

. . . our said sovereign lord, his heirs and successors kings of this realm, shall have full power and authority from time to time to visit, repress, redress, reform, order, correct, restrain and amend all such errors, heresies, abuses, offences, contempts and enormities, whatsoever they be.

Act of Supremacy, 1534

Necessity is the plea for every infringement of human freedom. It is the argument of tyrants; it is the creed of slaves.

William Pitt the Younger, 1783

The tree of liberty must be refreshed from time to time with the blood of patriots and tyrants. It is its natural manure.

Thomas Jefferson, 1787

People demand freedom of speech as a compensation for the freedom of thought which they seldom use.

Søren Kierkegaard

Let's find out what everyone is doing. And then stop
everyone from doing it.
A. P. Herbert

If a chap doesn't like a file being kept on him, there's
usually a very good reason and that's just the kind of
chap we should be keeping files on.
Harold Salsbury, former chief constable, quoted in the *Daily Telegraph*,
1991

Help the police. Beat yourself up.
Graffito, Mornington Crescent station, c. 1979

They that can give up essential liberty to obtain a little
safety deserve neither liberty nor safety.
Benjamin Franklin

This remains a country where causing embarrassment is
the highest treason, where concern for the facts lies not
in what they contain but how they got out, and where
the only victims of the truth are those who tell it.
Keith Waterhouse on the jailing of Whitehall whistle-blower Sarah
Tisdall, 1983

People must not do things for fun. We are not here for
fun. There is no reference to fun in any Act of Parliament.
A. P. Herbert

While there are always arguments available in support of suppressing speech, society is almost always better served when those arguments are rejected.

Professor Floyd Abrams, 2005

They took away my liberty but not my freedom.

Brian Keenan, hostage in Beirut 1986–1990

One word almost never appears – and never in a central place – in all these speeches and pamphlets and books about the Third Way: liberty . . . This is no accident. The Third Way is not about either open societies or liberty. There is, indeed, a curious authoritarian streak in it.

Ralf Dahrendorf, *Foreign Affairs*, 1999

Life and Death

Inter faeces et urinas nascimur
(We are all born between piss and shit)
St Augustine

All life is a shit sandwich, and every day I take
another bite.
Attr. Joe Schmidt, American football coach

We have to go through life with the air of quiet
expectancy which belongs to the motorist parked on a
double yellow line.
Roy Clarke, *Last of the Summer Wine*

A sigh between two secrets.
Attr. Peg Sayers, story-teller, of Great Blasket Island, Co. Kerry

The Dark Night of the Soul.
Title of a work by St John of the Cross

In a real dark night of the soul it is always three o'clock in
the morning.
Scott Fitzgerald, *The Crack-up*

All moanday, tearsday, wailsday, thumpsday, frightday,
shatterday till the fear of the Law.
James Joyce, *Finnegans Wake*

It is one of the strange discoveries a man can make
that life, however you lead it, contains moments of
exhilaration; there are always comparisons that can
be made with worse times; even in danger and misery
the pendulum swings.
Graham Greene, *The Power and the Glory*

It is one of the secrets of Nature in its mood of mockery
that fine weather lays a heavier weight on the mind
and hearts of the depressed and the inwardly tormented
than does a really bad day with dark rain snivelling
continuously and sympathetically from a dark sky.
Muriel Spark, *Territorial Rights*

Literature is mostly about having sex and not much
about having children. Life is the other way around.
David Lodge

Middle age comes upon one suddenly, like a traffic ticket.
Darryl Pinckney

Life is like invading Russia. A blitz start, massed shakos,
plumes dancing like a flustered henhouse; a period of
svelte progress recorded in ebullient despatches as the
enemy falls back; then the beginning of a long morale-
sapping trudge with rations getting shorter and the first
snowflakes on your face. The enemy burns Moscow and

you yield to General January, whose fingernails are very
icicles. Bitter retreat. Harrying Cossacks. Eventually you
fall beneath a boy-gunner's grapeshot while crossing
some Polish river not even marked on your general's map.
Julian Barnes, *Talking It Over*

'The thing about getting older,' said Chanu, 'is that you
don't need everything to be possible any more, you just
need some things to be certain.'
Monica Ali, *Brick Lane*

Everyone goes on about the quality of life these days.
I can't see what's wrong with old-fashioned quantity.
Ronald Higgins

If the executioner were to offer me five minutes for a
quick smoke before I ascended the gallows then I would
choose the five minutes that booksellers are going to be
back in, despite the proven scientific chance of my
getting lung cancer before I was hanged.
'Drif', connoisseur of second-hand bookshops, *Oldie*, 1992

And even in our sleep, pain that cannot forget falls drop
by drop upon the heart, and in our own despair, against
our will, comes wisdom to us by the awful grace of God.
**Aeschylus, quoted by Robert Kennedy on the night of Martin Luther
King's assassination, 1968, two months before his own**

She thought what people seem generally to think when they first get wind of someone else's catastrophe: how does this affect me? So-and-so in my office has a brain tumour? That means I have to take inventory alone. So-and-so from next door went down on that plane? He died in that crash? No, it can't be. He was coming over on Saturday to fix our garbage disposal.

Philip Roth, *I Married A Communist*

. . . the cows and calves of bygone years now gone to an oblivion almost inconceivable in its profundity.

Thomas Hardy, *Tess of the d'Urbervilles*

Maintenant, elle est comme les autres.

General de Gaulle, on the death of his daughter Anne, who had Down's syndrome, 1948

The trees they do grow high
    And the leaves they do grow green
But the time has gone and passed, my love
    That you and I have seen.

It's a cold winter's night, my love,
    And you and I must bide alone.
The bonny lad was young
    But a-growing.

Traditional

Do you know who has just been sitting where you are, sir, Lord Bertrand Russell, the philosopher. But when I asked him, 'Well, Lord Russell, what's it all about, then?', do you know, guv, he didn't know!

London taxi-driver, quoted in the *Guardian*, 1992

Those whom the gods love, die young.

Menander (342 – c. 292 BC)

I am waiting for you for an interval, somewhere very near, just around the corner. All is well.

Canon Henry Scott Holland

What can we say when we consider the loss of a friend, a colleague, a mentor? How do we express the sense of loss, the grief, the awful longing for what might have been? There is a way. We do it with a word, a simple word, a word we all recognize. It is a word that enters the lives of us all. It is a word that expresses emotions across the whole enormous gamut of human feelings, a word that touches all of our loves as well as all of our griefs. What shall we say when we consider that Hugh has gone? We shall say the word and the word is . . . FUCK!

Eulogy by Dibbs Mather for Australian author Hugh Atkinson, reported by Philip Knightley, *A Hack's Progress*

I made myself laugh at everything for fear of having to weep.

Beaumarchais

Il a creusé notre tombe en mourant
He has dug our tomb by dying
**Stéphane Mallarmé, *For Anatole's Tomb* [notes for a poem – never
written – on the death of his eight-year-old son]**

*Famille parfaite. Équilibre père fils mère fille rompu – trois,
    un vide entre nous, cherchant.*
Perfect family. Father son mother daughter broken – three, a
    void between us, searching.
Ibid.

*Père qui né en temps mauvais – avait préparé à fils – une
    tâche sublime – a la double à remplir . . . la douleur le
    défie de se sacrifier à qui n'est plus – l'emportera-t-elle
    sur vigeur (homme qu'il n'a pas été) et fera-t-il la tâche
    de l'enfant.*
Father who was born in a bad time – having prepared for son
    – a sublime task – has the double one to fulfil . . . the
    sadness challenges him to sacrifice himself for the one who
    has gone – will it triumph over strength (the man Anatole
    did not become) and will he do the child's task.
Ibid.

*Il est une époque de l'Existence où nous nous retrouverons,
    sinon un lieu*
There is a time in existence in which we will find each other
    again, if not a place.
Ibid.

This much I'm reasonably certain of, that there are much worse emotions to have to live with than sadness, however vast and deep that sadness might be. It can be uplifting, invigorating, strengthening, motivating and, above all, a powerful reminder of how much Laurie still matters, and always will. It can be other things, too, but don't let it.

Jon Henderson, in a letter of condolence to the Engel family, 2005

I know your sorrow and I know that for the likes of us there is no ease to be had from words of reason and that in the very assurance of sorrow's fading there is more sorrow. So I offer you my deeply affectionate and compassionate thoughts and wish for you only that the strange thing may never fail you, whatever it is, that gives us the strength to live on and on with our wounds.

Samuel Beckett

Life is not a journey towards happiness, it's a journey towards understanding.

Fay Weldon

London

Hell is a city much like London.
Shelley

Over the centuries various addresses rose and fell in
dignity. West Cheap, Chancery Lane, the Strand, Covent
Garden – each had its day and then slid downmarket
or was redeveloped. But the great Georgian estates
have remained (with their clones, such as Belgravia or
Kensington) the chic places to live, shop, saunter and
dine. Town remained tops. Unlike Birmingham's
Edgbaston and Manchester's Didsbury, no Victorian
suburb eclipsed the West End.
Roy Porter, *London: A Social History*

It is a curious but well-known fact that bugs are much
commoner in south than north London.
George Orwell, *Down and Out in Paris and London*

'All they said was they wanted to preserve the original.'
'Well, you can make the original again, can't you?'
Builders gentrifying Battishill Street, Islington, 1980

Perhaps the noblest of all my conceptions. A revival of
the arrogance of the old mediaeval cities applied to our

glorious suburbs. Clapham with a city guard. Wimbledon with a city wall. Surbiton tolling the bell to raise its citizens. West Hampstead going into battle with its own banner.

G. K. Chesterton, *The Napoleon of Notting Hill*

. . . when the LCC began to expand the Downham Estate, near Bromley, local residents objected at an inquiry saying: 'Such a scheme will reduce the respectability of the . . . streets by inundating the neighbourhood with working classes.' In fact, in 1925 the sensitive residents of a private estate which abutted the southern edge of Downham took the law into their own hands and actually built a brick wall [about 7 ft tall] across a road that led straight from the private part of the street to the council houses. Bromley Council refused to co-operate with LCC demands for its demolition, and it was not pulled down until the early years of the Second World War when it impeded emergency services.

Gavin Weightman and Steve Humphries, *The Making of Modern London, 1914–1939*

Our Father,
Who art in Hendon
Harrow Road be Thy name
Thy Kingston come
Thy Wimbledon
In Erith as it is in Hendon.

Give us this day our Berkhamsted
And forgive us our Westminsters
As we forgive those who Westminster against us.
Lead us not into Temple Station
And deliver us from Ealing,
For thine is the Kingston
The Purley and the Crawley,
For Iver and Iver
Crouch End

'The Bus Driver's Prayer', from *The Bus Driver's Prayer and Other Stories*
by Ian Dury (1992)

. . . the capital – that strange hybrid of Londhattan and Londonistan – has never been less British. Enriched by the growth of international financial services, populated by immigrants from the four corners of the globe, London is to the UK what Hong Kong is to the People's Republic of China.

Niall Ferguson, *Sunday Telegraph*, 2006

Genghis Khan could rape and pillage his way across Camden with impunity, but if his yak strayed one inch from a parking bay he would be found swinging from a lamppost with a parking ticket in his mouth.

Simon Jenkins, *Guardian*, 2006

In 1791 Horace Walpole complained that the growth of the city was killing the sedan-chair trade; Soho became the centre of the nightclub trade after restaurants were banned from serving officers alcohol after 10 p.m. under the 'Beauty Sleep order' in the First World War; the first conversion of a MAYFAIR stable into a bijou mews house was in 1908; HAMPSTEAD HEATH remained an open space because its owner, Sir Thomas Maryon Wilson, uniquely failed to get an act through Parliament allowing him to develop it; in the early 1930s new brick houses were available on the Heathway Park Estate in MITCHAM for £315 and in SIDCUP for £250 (£5 deposit); £500 was an average suburban price.

Love, Beauty and a Bit of the Other

'You've got that Gilchrist woman all wrong – she doesn't just jump into bed with anybody.'

People who haven't learned to love someone else better than they love themselves, I say they haven't begun to live.

Catherine Bramwell-Booth, Salvation Army commissioner, aged one hundred, 1983

Tammy Wynette demanded an apology from Hillary Clinton for saying she was not 'some little woman, standing by my man, like Tammy Wynette'. So did her fifth husband.

Reported in *USA Today*, 1992

'I don't believe,' said Mr Prendergast, 'that people would ever fall in love or want to be married if they hadn't been told about it. It's like abroad. Nobody would want to go there if they hadn't been told it existed.'

Evelyn Waugh, *Decline and Fall*

Love may or may not produce happiness; whether or not it does in the end, its primary effect is to energize. Have you ever talked as well, needed less sleep, returned to sex so eagerly, as when you were first in love? The anaemic begin to glow, while the normally healthy become intolerable. Next, it gives spine-stretching confidence. You feel you are standing up straight for the first time in your life; you feel you can do anything while this feeling lasts, you can take on the world. (Shall we make this distinction: that love enhances the confidence, whereas sexual conquest merely develops the ego?)

Julian Barnes, *A History of the World in 10½ Chapters*

If they like your little jokes before you're married, afterwards they ask why you're always trying to be funny.

J. B. Priestley, play: *Eden End* (1934)

What is it with women that as soon as you fall in love with a guy you want to take him in for alterations?
Musical: *Guys and Dolls* (1955)

I had such plans for you, Carter, I could just visualise you all chunky and manly and lantern-jawed just like one of them husbands you see on the front of the knitting patterns . . . I used to visualise you coming home from work with a smug grin on your face because you'd just beaten a chief systems analyst at squash and you'd glide into the kitchen and you'd put your arms round me waist and you'd croon: 'Oh, darling, are we having real custard again with the ratatouille?'
Peter Tinniswood, *I Didn't Know You Cared*

What I did not know – I was a young man – is that there are two kinds of love. The kind that starts off big and slowly wears away, that seems you can never use it up and then one day it is finished. And the kind that you don't notice at first, but which adds a little bit to itself every day, like an oyster makes a pearl, grain by grain, a jewel from the sand.
Monica Ali, *Brick Lane*

Few men do understand the nature of a woman's heart, till years have robbed such understanding of its value.
Anthony Trollope, *Barchester Towers*

Jealousy is always born with love, but does not always die with it.

François de Marsillac, Duc de La Rochefoucauld, *Maxims*

'Even now,' she [Madre Mia] thought, 'almost no one remembers Esteban and Pepita, but myself. Camila also remembers her uncle Pio and her son; this woman, her mother. But soon we shall die and all memory of those five will have left the earth and we ourselves shall be loved for a while and forgotten. But the love will have been enough; all those impulses of love return to the love that made them. There is a land of the living and a land of the dead, and the bridge is love, the only survival, the only meaning.'

Thornton Wilder, *The Bridge of San Luis Rey*

GRANT, Rose. Beloved mother of Linda and Michele and dear grandma of Ben, on October 15, in London, after a long illness bravely borne. She taught her daughters to respect others, that chicken soup cures almost everything and that a good handbag makes the outfit. May she rest in peace.

Announcement, *Jewish Chronicle*, 1999

Father Nikolai always dressed in black with a black beard. For years I thought he was an Italian widow.

Woody Allen, film: *Love and Death* (1975)

If you've got tits, you don't go and work for the council.
Alan Bennett, *Enjoy*

The humbler one's concept of beauty, the more likely one
is to find it.
Margaret Drabble

Give me a few minutes to talk away my face and I can
seduce the Queen of France.
Voltaire

Why tease the vultures?
Joan Rivers on sunbathing

'Dear me, when I went to balls,' said an Edwardian
beauty mystified by the modern use of deodorants,
'the gentlemen used to *like* what we called a *bouquet
de corsage*.'
Alison Adburgham, *Shops and Shopping 1800–1914*

He said Do you want it pasteurized? 'Cos pasteurized
     is best,
She says Ernie, I'll be happy if it comes up to
     my chest.
Benny Hill, 'Ernie (The Fastest Milkman in the West)'

Screwing around is fooling around without dinner.
Musical: *Chicago* (1975)

We stood on the bridge at midnight,
My heart was all a-quiver.
I undid her suspender belt
And her leg fell in the river.
Anon.

Greeks of the classical period attached no importance
to the biological sex of the object of a man's desire.
Boys and women were equally acceptable: what
mattered was who performed the active sexual role ...
the whole relationship was thus primarily one of power
and of its natural hierarchy. It was assumed that men
were naturally attracted both to women and good-
looking boys; for an adult male person to be penetrated
sexually by another was a disgrace to him but to perform
the act on a boy was not shameful.
New York Review of Books, 1990

Not only did you do something disgusting, you did it with
a boy from another house.
Julian Mitchell, *Another Country*

... within days of arriving, he had achieved what Guy
Burgess failed to do in almost five years, locating the one
gentlemen's lavatory in central Moscow where pick-ups
could be had.
Francis Wheen, *Tom Driberg*

'He died of natural causes.'
'Your respected headmaster got his sexual thrills from
    wearing armour and being strung up on a rope.
    You call that natural causes?'
'It was natural to him.'
David Nobbs, *Pratt of the Argus*

That's my Dick. Always standing up for a fellow.
Attr. G. A. Henty

WALLY: They do say as the Japanese are gifted in the
    trickier practices of the marriage bed.
CLEGG: All that means in this part of the world is knowing
    how to secure more than your fair share of the
    eiderdown.
Roy Clarke, *Last of the Summer Wine*

In the second century, the great Gnostic master
Valentinus resolved the damnable dilemma by claiming
that Jesus 'ate and drank but did not defecate' . . . In the
fourth century St Jerome completely rejected the notion
that Adam and Eve had sexual intercourse in Paradise.
On the other hand, Johannes Scotus Erigena, the great
ninth-century theologian, accepted the idea. He believed,
moreover, that Adam's virile member could be made to
rise like an arm or a leg, when and as its owner wished.
We must not dismiss this fancy as the recurrent dream of

a man obsessed with the threat of impotence, Erigena's idea has a different meaning. If it were possible to raise the penis by means of a simple command, then sexual excitement would have no place in the world. What the great theologian found incompatible with Paradise was not sexual intercourse and the attendant pleasure; what he found incompatible with Paradise was excitement.

Milan Kundera, *The Unbearable Lightness of Being*

In an exuberant letter of 1877, Guy de Maupassant informed a friend that a physician had attributed his loss of hair and related symptoms to syphilis and put him on a regime of mercury and potassium iodine. Then a twenty-seven-year-old writer acquiring a reputation for brilliant, worldly – many said obscene – short stories and a libertine of almost legendary capacities, he was glad to hear it. His hair, he reported, was growing back and he was feeling very well. 'I've got the pox! At last! The real thing! Not the contemptible clap . . . no – no – the great pox, the one which Francis I died of. The majestic pox, pure and simple, the elegant syphilis . . . I am proud of it by thunder, and to hell with the bourgeoisie.' In his exhilaration he repeated himself: 'Hallelujah, I've got the pox, so I don't have to worry about catching it any more, and I screw the street whores and trollops, and afterwards I say to them, "I've got the pox." They are afraid and I just laugh.' Some years after this eruption, he entered what physicians were beginning to recognise

as the tertiary stage of the disease, went mad tortured
by horrifying delusions, and died. He was forty-two.
Peter Gay, *Schnitzler's Century*

A recent survey showed that men have sex 1.51 times a
week and women 1.26 times.
***Daily Telegraph*, 1991**

In our hearts there is a ruthless dictator, ready to
contemplate the misery of a thousand strangers if it
will ensure the happiness of the few we love.
Graham Greene, *The Heart of the Matter*

Jenny kiss'd me when we met
    Jumping from the chair she sat in.
Time, you thief, who love to get
    Sweets into your list, put that in!
Say I'm weary, say I'm sad,
    Say that health and wealth have miss'd me,
Say I'm growing old, but add,
    Jenny kiss'd me.
Leigh Hunt, 'Rondeau'

I wasn't kissing her. I was whispering in her mouth.
Chico Marx

'Remember, this gun is pointed right at your heart.'
'That is my least vulnerable spot.'
Film: *Casablanca* (1942)

'What have been the effects of leading the Greater
    London Council on your health and physique,
    Mr Livingstone?'
'There has been the most *enormous* swelling of my
    genitalia.'
Ken Livingstone, interview with *Time Out*, 1985

Whenever I meet prostitutes, they never speak of sex,
they enquire about the soul and about God. I also meet
many ascetics and monks, and whenever we are alone,
they ask about nothing but sex.
Acharya Rajneesh

There are only two certainties in life: death and nurses.
John Francome

Outside every thin girl, there's a fat man trying to get in.
Katharine Whitehorn

You think getting a blow job from a big-bosomed
twenty-six-year-old is a pleasure to me?
Woody Allen, film: *Deconstructing Harry* (1997)

Erotic is when you do something imaginative and
sensitive with a feather. Kinky is when you use the whole
chicken.
Attr. Elmore Leonard

From a South African lonely hearts column: 'Single black female seeks male companionship, ethnicity unimportant. I'm a good-looking girl who loves to play. I love long walks in the wood, riding in your 4x4, hunting, camping, barbecues, and cosy winter nights lying by the fire. Candlelight dinners will have me eating out of your hand. Rub me the right way and watch me respond. I'll be at the front door when you get home from work, wearing only what nature gave me. Call xxx xxxx and ask for Lady Jane.' Over 300 excited men called and found themselves talking to the Society for the Prevention of Cruelty to Animals about an eight-week-old black Labrador.

Press Gazette, 2002

The only guaranteed result of having an affair would be to add yet another disapproving woman to his life.

Jonathan Franzen, *The Corrections*

The rule of thumb for male full-frontals is the angle of the Mull of Kintyre to the mainland.

Editor, *For Women* magazine, quoted in the *Guardian*, 1998

She touched his organ, and from that bright epoch even it, the old companion of his happiest hours, incapable as he had thought of elevation, began a new and deified existence.

Charles Dickens, *Martin Chuzzlewit*

You could know everything there was in the world and yet if you were ignorant of that one dirty scramble you know nothing.
Graham Greene, *Brighton Rock*

She tells me that she thought I was cute, a word that no one has ever previously used in connection with me, and soulful, by which I think she means that I don't say much and I always look vaguely pissed off.
Nick Hornby, *High Fidelity*

Dachshunds and erections can't climb stairs.
Les Barker

The lobby of the House of Commons is the third easiest place to get picked up in Europe after Funland in Leicester Square and the arrivals lounge at Rome Airport.
Alan Clark

Upset? Certainly not. It's like being unchained from a lunatic.
Socrates, on losing his sex drive

The female Barbary macaque does it with a different partner every 17 minutes ... marsupial mice bang away for 13 hours ... Don Giovanni's 1,003 conquests pale into insignificance compared to the pied flycatcher.
Jared Diamond, *Why Is Sex Fun?*

H. G. Wells told Willie [Somerset Maugham] that he could not write unless he had sex with a woman after lunch and before dinner every day. 'And what do you do after tea?' Willie enquired drily.

Bryan Connon, *Somerset Maugham and the Maugham Dynasty*

Nature

Four million different kinds of animals and plants in the world. Four million different solutions to the problem of staying alive.
David Attenborough, *Planet Earth*

Elephants use infrasonic and possibly even seismic communication to send messages to their family members across distances as great as twenty-five miles ... male chimpanzees wage territorial wars in just the same way as humans do, resulting in many deaths ... the stereotypically friendly dolphin has been observed to engage in gang-rape of an isolated female.
Review in the *Guardian* of Temple Grandin and Catherine Johnson,
***Animals in Translation*, 2005**

Earthmen are not proud of their ancestors and never invite them round for dinner.
Douglas Adams, *The Hitchhiker's Guide to the Galaxy*

One creature that very much featured in the lives of the early colonists was the passenger pigeon ... One early observer estimated a passing flock as being a mile wide and 240 miles long. They literally darkened the sky. At the time of the *Mayflower* landing there were perhaps nine billion passenger pigeons in North America, more than twice the number of all birds on the Continent today. With such numbers they were absurdly easy to hunt. One account of 1770 reported that a hunter brought down 125 with a single shot from a blunderbuss. Some people ate them, but most were fed to pigs. Millions more were slaughtered for the sport of it . . . On 1 September 1914, the last one died at Cincinnati Zoo.

Bill Bryson, *Made in America*

The [zebra-like] quagga roamed the plains of the Karoo in vast herds. Then European settlers arrived . . . the last remaining quagga, a captive mare, died forlorn and unnoticed on 12 August 1883 in Amsterdam Zoo. Such was the ignorance of the quagga's plight at that time that the Cape authorities issued a proclamation to protect the species two years after it had become extinct.

Daily Telegraph, 2006

Onagers have never been domesticated . . . zebras are even worse. Efforts at domestication went as far as hitching them to carts: they were tried out as draft animals in nineteenth-century South Africa, and the eccentric Lord Walter Rothschild drove through the streets of London in a carriage pulled by zebras. Alas, zebras become impossibly dangerous as they grow older

... [and] have the unpleasant habit of biting a person and not letting go. They thereby injure even more American zookeepers than do tigers. Zebras are also virtually impossible to lasso ... because of their unfailing ability to watch the rope noose fly toward them and then to duck their head out of the way.

Jared Diamond, *Guns, Germs and Steel*

If people died the way mayflies do, we'd probably leave the world less protestingly. Until its last day of life, the immature mayfly clings to a rock at the bottom of a trout stream. On that last day, something wonderful happens. The mayfly nymph hatches out of its lobsterlike skin, sprouts beautiful diaphanous wings, takes to the air on a lovely spring afternoon, finds a mate, copulates for the first and only time, lays its eggs and drops dead, tired but satisfied.

Peter Kaminsky, *New York Times*, 1991

Millions of newly-identified animals still require names. A Smithsonian researcher named Terry Erwin, whose speciality is ground beetles of the genus *Agra*, named one very difficult species *Agra vation* ... There's a fly called *Phthira relativitae* and a wasp called *Heerz lukenatcha* ... Naming rights to a Bolivian monkey were bought by a Canadian online casino in 2005 for $650,000. It became

Callicebus aureipalatii, the Golden Palace monkey. Also, in 2005 two Republican coleoptorists named beetles *Agathidium bushi*, *A. cheneyi* and *A. rumsfeldi*. Democrats noted these beetles lived on slime mould . . .

Sting has his own tree frog, *Hyla stingi*. Spiders include *Calponia harrisonfordi* and *Pachygnatha zappa*. Other additions include: *Colon rectum* (a beetle), *Ba humbugi* (a snail), *Oedipus complex* (a snail), *Ytu brutus* (a beetle) and *Trombicula fujigmo* – a mite, whose name is an acronym for Fuck you, Jack, I've got my orders.

International Herald Tribune, 1996 / The Economist, 2006

One greenfly on a leaf at the start of spring would, if every one lived to maturity and avoided disease, ladybirds and blue tits, turn into 1000 million tons of greenfly by autumn.

Stefan Buczacki, *Gardeners' Question Time*, 1988

Wasps are not really pests at all: they play a vital role in pollinating fruit and flowers, and keeping down blackfly and greenfly. The trouble comes when nests break up towards the end of summer, and up to 30,000 worker wasps with a taste for sugar and no further role in life are unleashed from each nest like football hooligans on an unsuspecting world.

Independent, 1990

SPECIES DECLARED EXTINCT 1984–2004

ANIMALS

Class	Species	Common name	Home
Amphibian	*Atelopus ignescens*	Jambato toad	Ecuador
Amphibian	*Atelopus longirostris*		Ecuador
Amphibian	*Bufo periglenes*	golden toad	Costa Rica
Amphibian	*Eleutherodactylus chrysozetetes*		Honduras
Amphibian	*Eleutherodactylus milesi*		Honduras
Amphibian	*Rheobatrachus vitellinus*	northern gastric brooding frog	Australia
Amphibian	*Cynops wolterstorffi*	Yunnan Lake newt	China
Bird	*Moho braccatus*	Kauai 'O'o	Hawaii
Bird	*Podilymbus gigas*	Atitlán grebe	Guatemala
Bird	*Myadestes myadestinus*	Kama'o	Hawaii

PLANTS

Class	Species	Common name	Home
Magnoliopsida	*Cyanea dolichopoda*	haha	Hawaii
Magnoliopsida	*Argyroxiphium virescens*	silversword	Hawaii
Magnoliopsida	*Crudia zeylanica*		Sri Lanka
Magnoliopsida	*Nesiota elliptica*	St Helena olive	St Helena
Magnoliopsida	*Oldenlandia adscenionis*		Ascension

World Conservation Union, 2006
[Many more species have probably become extinct – some of which might have contained cures for cancer or other diseases – over the past two decades. But the criteria for determining extinction are exacting. And of the possible 16 million species on the planet, only 1.8 million have been properly described.]

A single female APHID, Phylloxera vastatrix, *which destroyed the vines of France in the 1860s, can produce 25.6 billion descendants in eight months without any male assistance . . . The* WREN *is said to be the commonest British bird, with seven million pairs nesting every year, but according to a British Trust for Ornithology survey in*

2004, it was only the fourth most seen, behind the WOOD PIGEON, CHAFFINCH and BLACKBIRD . . . A young SWIFT may fly continuously for three years; a pair of KINGFISHERS can catch up to 115 fish a day; it is claimed that news of the Battle of Jutland in 1916 was the agitated calls of PHEASANT in East Anglia; the SCOTTISH CROSSBILL, from the Highland pine forests, is now regarded as the only bird species found solely in the UK; after a long debate among ornithologists it was decided in 2006 it had a 'Scottish accent' that made it distinct from all other crossbills . . . the ARCTIC TERN has the longest migration of any creature on earth and sees more daylight than any other – some birds go from the Arctic to the Antarctic . . . the PRONGHORN ANTELOPE of the American West is the world's second fastest animal at 61 mph, 9 mph behind the cheetah . . . tiny crayfish, the BAIKAL EPISHURA, live in Lake Baikal at a density estimated at up to three million per square metre of the lake's surface . . . the only wild LADY'S SLIPPER ORCHID in the UK is in a single guarded location in Wharfedale, Yorkshire . . . the FINGERED SPEEDWELL may now be confined to a new housing estate in Thetford, Norfolk; MARTIN'S RAMPING FUMITORY grows on a couple of sites near Truro and an allotment on the Isle of Wight . . . There are over a million known species of INSECTS and possibly ten million unknown . . . one estimate is that for every living person there are two-hundred million insects . . . according to a 1943 study, an acre of Cambridgeshire pasture can support over 400 million insects, 666 million MITES and 38 million

CENTIPEDES and MILLIPEDES ... The DESERT LOCUST forms swarms comprising an estimated ten to twenty-five billion insects ... Something like two hundred and fifty tons of insects are eaten every night by the twenty million BATS in the Bracken Cave, Central Texas ... A GIANT PANDA eats up to a hundred pounds of bamboo shoots a day ... The AMAZON carries as much fresh water as the world's next six (maybe ten) biggest rivers combined ... Every year the PARANÁ River, South America, floods an area the size of England ... There are two or three million TERMITES in a hill; a queen termite produces thirty thousand eggs a day ... NILE PERCH, introduced to Lake Victoria in the 1950s, wiped out an estimated two hundred local species; and the planes exporting them reportedly help bring in guns to help wipe out humans ... The BROWN TREE SNAKE arrived in Guam from Papua New Guinea in military equipment in the 1950s and has now wiped out twelve of the fourteen local bird species ... POLAR BEAR liver is poisonous.

The News Business

'I'm going on maternity leave to have Elvis's love child.'

If your mother says she loves you, check it out.
Newsroom motto, Chicago City News Service, closed 2005

We are in a great hurry to construct a magnetic telegraph from Maine to Texas; but Maine and Texas, it may be, have nothing important to communicate . . . We are eager to tunnel under the Atlantic and bring the old world some weeks nearer to the new; but perchance the first news that will leak through into the broad flapping American ear will be that Princess Adelaide has the whooping cough.

H. D. Thoreau, *Walden*

In the newspaper game 1918 was the year that sealed the pre-eminence of speed over thought. Roy Howard of United Press reported the end of World War I three days early and, instead of getting the sack, rose to heights seldom scaled in the industry. It was an omen.

A. J. Liebling, *The Press*

An editor is one who separates the wheat from the chaff and prints the chaff.

Adlai Stevenson

I knew it wasn't him. It's never him, never the journalist – always the bloody sub, and if it's not the sub it's the editor. And if it's not the editor, it's the owner, and if it's not the owner, it's a typing error. Makes you puke.

Neil Kinnock, on being misquoted by the *Daily Star*, 1987

You don't pick up a tabloid to find out about the sisal crop in Malaysia. The best story of any type in a tabloid is murder at a good address.

Pete Hamill, quoted in the *New York Times*, 2006

But Rupert, Rupert, your readers are my shoplifters.

Bloomingdale's executive responding to complaint by Mr Murdoch about the store's failure to advertise in the *New York Post*, quoted in the *Guardian*, 1983

The archetypal tabloid story is a piece of high-precision engineering, with the predictability accurate to within 1/1000th of an inch, the hackneyed phraseology polished like old brass, and puns worn smooth with age gliding effortlessly into place like the moving parts of a well-oiled Victorian donkey engine.

Keith Waterhouse

The purpose of a newspaper is not to educate but to startle.

James Gordon Bennett

Why couldn't it have been the Staten Island Ferry?

Than Van Ranck, night editor of the *New York American*, on hearing 932 had died on a ferry in the Yangtze, c. 1930

The *News Chronicle* [d. 1960] died of an embolism: a wholesome circulation impeded by clots.

James Cameron

By gentlemen for gentlemen.

W. M. Thackeray on the *Pall Mall Gazette*

By office boys for office boys.
Lord Salisbury on the *Daily Mail*

To work in Fleet Street and never to have served on the
Express is like being a soldier and never having heard
the sound of gunfire.
Brian Inglis

When despatching me to be a war correspondent in
Abyssinia in 1935, the editor [of the *Morning Post*],
H. A. Gwynne, tendered three bits of advice. Please
remember a dead correspondent is valueless. A finger of
whisky in a water-bottle kills bugs . . . and get all your
clothes from a decent outfitter. You're representing *us*.
W. F. Deedes, *Sunday Telegraph*, 1993

News is what someone somewhere doesn't want
published. All the rest is advertising.
Lord Northcliffe

Advertisements in a newspaper are more truthful than
the news pages. On the news pages aeroplanes crash and
houses burn down, bringing disaster and bereavement.
In the adverts, planes land safely and punctually, uniting
families who live in warm, comfortable houses. Which is
truer of everyday life?
Peregrine Worsthorne, quoted in the *Guardian*, 1993

Why don't you start a vendetta against somebody? That's the way to get people reading your column.
Lord Beaverbrook

The first thing a reporter has to learn is to keep his eyes and ears open and his mouth shut.
T. Campbell Copeland, *Ladder to Journalism*, 1889

Generally speaking, the best people nowadays go into journalism, the second best into business, the rubbish goes into politics and the shits into law.
Auberon Waugh, 1981

The only qualities essential for real success in journalism are ratlike cunning, a plausible manner, and a little literary ability. The ratlike cunning is needed to ferret out and publish things that people don't want to be known (which is – and always will be – the best definition of News). The plausible manner is useful for surviving while this is going on, helpful with the entertaining presentation of it, and even more useful in later life when the successful journalist may have to become a successful executive on his newspaper. The literary ability is of obvious use.

Other qualities are helpful, but not diagnostic. These include a knack with telephones, trains, and petty officials; a good digestion and a steady head; total recall; enough idealism to inspire indignant prose (but not enough to inhibit detached professionalism); a paranoid temperament; an ability to believe passionately in second-rate objects; well-placed relatives; the willingness to betray, if not friends, acquaintances.

A reluctance to understand too much too well (because *tout comprendre c'est tout pardonner*, and *tout pardonner* makes dull copy); an implacable hatred of spokesmen, administrators, lawyers, public relations men, politicians, and all those who would rather pervert words than policies; and the strength to lead a disrupted personal life without going absolutely haywire. The capacity to steal other people's ideas and phrases – that one about ratlike cunning was invented by my colleague Murray Sayle – is also invaluable.

Nicholas Tomalin, *Sunday Times*, 1969

Q: What's pink and hard in the morning?
A: The *Financial Times* crossword.

Anon.

Sir Larry Lamb [editor of the *Sun*] . . . Knight of the Garter, the exotic bra, the frilly knickers and the novelty suspender belt.

Roy Hattersley, *Punch*, 1983

People who can't write interviewing people who can't talk for people who can't read.

Frank Zappa on rock journalism

A ball player never recalls a reporter's face on less than six introductions or his name on less than twenty.
Ring Lardner

A sports writer ... someone who would if he could, but he can't, so he tells those who can how they should.
Cliff Temple

Between 1958 and 1972 the Queen was pregnant 92 times, had 149 accidents and nine miscarriages [according to French newspapers] and took the pill 11 times. She abdicated 63 times and was on the point of breaking up with Prince Philip 73 times. She was said to be fed up 112 times and on the verge of a nervous breakdown 32 times. She had 43 unhappy nights, 27 nightmares and her life was threatened 29 times. She was rude to the Queen of Persia 11 times, to Princess Grace of Monaco six times and to Queen Fabiola only twice, and she expelled Lord Snowdon from Court 151 times.
Henry Porter, *Lies, Damned Lies and Some Exclusives*, 1984

I know with what cavalier disdain even the ostensibly serious aspects of newspapers are regarded by those who never had to try to form a thought at any time, least of all under pressure of a looming deadline, a thirst, a ringing phone and an uneasy conscience. It is rather sad that we should ever imagine it otherwise. It is salutary to recognize the inconsequential nature of one's accomplishment.

James Cameron

News is what a chap who doesn't care much about anything wants to read, and it's only news until he's read it, after which it's dead.

Evelyn Waugh, *Scoop*

I wandered around beneath gloomy street lights, looking in shop windows, and reading those strange posters – bills, as they are known in the trade – that you always find for provincial newspapers. I have an odd fascination for these because they are always either wholly unfathomable to non-locals (LETTER BOX RAPIST STRIKES AGAIN. BEULAH FLIES HOME) or so boring that you can't imagine how anyone could possibly have thought they would boost sales (COUNCIL STORM OVER BINS CONTRACT, PHONE BOX VANDALS STRIKE AGAIN). My favourite – this is a real one, which I saw some years ago in Hemel Hempstead – was WOMAN, 81, DIES.

Bill Bryson, *Notes from a Small Island*

Raphael Dunvant was a man with the curious knack of catching the eye of *Daily Telegraph* journalists out for a kerbside quote. Patrolling the pavements, notebooks in hand, they kept bumping into him. Which was fortunate, as he always seemed to have something pithy and tangy to say. He lit up their stories. He did other things, too, worth recording. Once they found him on the fringe of some royal occasion dressed in a bin liner. On another occasion, his leg, which was made of metal, was struck by lightning – a story that greatly excited some television news editors, who did not, however, manage to trace him. Predictably, after the crowds turned violent after Scotland had played at Wembley [1988], it was Raphael who came up with a poignant tale of Caledonian brutality. These ruffians, it seemed, encountering him on a train north on his way to a salmon-fishing holiday, had broken poor Raphael's rod. And that was the end of Raphael Dunvant. For the story caught the eye of the formidable old editor of the *Sunday Express*, John Junor. From his fastness in Auchtermuchty, he sent a thunderous letter to the editor of the *Telegraph* challenging the authenticity of the story. No one, he said, except for a cad, and certainly no lover of salmon fishing such as Raphael claimed to be, would attempt such an expedition out of season. So Raphael and his quotable quotes . . . graced the *Telegraph*'s columns no more. Whether the readers noticed, goodness knows, but his passing was deeply mourned in the newsroom.

Smallweed (David McKie), *Guardian*, 1999

If society's susceptibility to misinformation is like AIDS, then web sites and internet news groups and electronic bulletin boards – a vast, thrilling, promiscuous commingling of facts with fabrications – could be its bath houses.

Kurt Anderson, *New Yorker*

. . . Impossible to exaggerate gravity of the situation here, but I will do my best.

Anon.

A specific and cherished, not to say colourful, glory of English football's once tranquil subculture is being harshly dismantled. Once upon a time, Pinks and Greens speckled the land. Even in my boyhood's cuddly Cotswold village of the 1940s, us foot-stamping addicts would gather in the after-tea gloom at Stonehouse post office, expectant for the van with the Citizen Pinks from Gloucester; sometimes, for a double fix, we'd then leg it across to the LMS station where a quire of Bristol Greens would be slung from the passing train. Once, under the one platform gaslight there, I saw a landgirl lustily snogging all over her impassive soldier chap as he studiedly read his Green 'Un over her passionately gyrating shoulders.

Frank Keating, *Guardian,* **2006**

I fancied journalism – I must have mentioned this – from the moment I saw Rosalind Russell perch on the news editor's desk and cross her legs with a silky slither like snakes mating. Her hat, against all laws of gravity, was on the side of her head. You did not associate her with gravity at all. That, I thought, will do me.

Nancy Banks-Smith, *Guardian*, **1994**

Only Connect

LEW WALLACE, the author of *Ben-Hur*, was a Union general in the Civil War, Governor of New Mexico Territory and US Minister to Turkey.

P. T. BARNUM was Mayor of Bridgeport, Connecticut in 1875–76, before discovering Tom Thumb and Jumbo and starting his circus.

JERRY SPRINGER was Mayor of Cincinnati, Ohio in 1977–78, before discovering sex and starting his circus.

Napoleon's wife the EMPRESS JOSEPHINE (born Rose Tascher) bred the tea rose, ancestor of most modern garden roses.

ADMIRAL VON TIRPITZ, creator of the German navy, sent his daughters to Cheltenham Ladies' College.

ALICE KEPPEL, Edward VII's mistress, was Camilla Parker-Bowles's great-grandmother.

The Wild West gunfighter BAT MASTERSON later became sports editor (and then company secretary) of the New York *Morning Telegraph*.

BALFOUR (later Conservative Prime Minister) taught ASQUITH (later Liberal Prime Minister) how to ride a bicycle – at Warwick Castle in 1900.

Russian composer ALEXANDER BORODIN was also Professor of Chemistry at St Petersburg Medical School, and is credited with discovering, in 1871, the importance of cholesterol.

JIMMY KENNEDY, who wrote 'Red Sails in the Sunset', 'The Teddy Bears' Picnic', 'We're Gonna Hang Out the Washing on the Siegfried Line' and 'The Hokey-Cokey', was best man at Denis Thatcher's first wedding.

CHARLES G. DAWES, Vice-President of the United States from 1925 to 1929, wrote 'Melody in A Major', which was later turned into 'Many a tear has to fall but it's all in the game'.

JACK B. TENNEY, composer of 'Mexicali Rose', ran for US Vice-President as candidate of the anti-Communist, anti-Semitic Christian Nationalist Party.

The actor RICKY TOMLINSON, star of *The Royle Family*, was one of the Shrewsbury Two, jailed for an illegal picket during a 1972 building strike.

WERNER KLEMPERER, Colonel Klink in *Hogan's Heroes*, was the son of the conductor Otto.

The reggae singer JUDGE DREAD, who had more UK reggae hits in the 1970s than even Bob Marley, was really a white man from Kent called Alex Hughes.

CÉZANNE and ZOLA went to school together in Aix-en-Provence and were great friends. (Cézanne reputedly won prizes for literature and Zola for drawing.)

The baby who Scarlett O'Hara drove in a buggy from a burning Atlanta was played by PATRICK CURTIS, who married Raquel Welch (some years later).

The heavyweight title fight between Bob Fitzsimmons and Tom Sharkey in San Francisco in 1896 was refereed by WYATT EARP, who controversially (and, according to rumour, corruptly) disqualified Fitzsimmons.

ADRIAN BELL, father of journalist and sometime MP Martin, compiled the first crossword in *The Times* in 1930.

The mobile-phone company NOKIA was previously famous for manufacturing galoshes.

The second and third Presidents of the US, JOHN ADAMS and THOMAS JEFFERSON, both died on 4 July 1826, the fiftieth anniversary of the Republic; ALDOUS HUXLEY and C. S. LEWIS died on 22 November 1963, when PRESIDENT KENNEDY was shot; the first *Dr Who* was shown on BBC

TV the next day. NIKITA KHRUSCHEV fell from power in Russia on the day HAROLD WILSON ousted the Conservatives in Britain by winning the General Election, 15 October 1964. FRANKIE HOWERD died on 19 April 1990; BENNY HILL, who was alone in his flat, probably did too.

To escape the opening battle of the Civil War, Bull Run, WILMER MCLEAN moved his family to the distant town of Appomattox Court House. Four years later, Lee surrendered to Grant in his front room. 'The war began in my front yard and ended in my front parlour,' McLean would say.

The site of Arlington National Cemetery was formerly ROBERT E. LEE's front garden. It was chosen, vengefully, during the Civil War.

JAMES CLARK MAXWELL, who established the laws of electromagnetism in 1873, was the boy known at Edinburgh Academy as 'Daftie'.

Playtime

If only Winston Churchill had called in the bookmakers' intelligence service to replace MI5, the war would have ended two years earlier.

Ryan Price, racehorse trainer

Homicides increase appreciably after every nationally broadcast heavyweight championship.

David Phillips, University of California sociologist, *New Republic*, 1988

Who is dis guy Queensberry? I don't see anything wrong with sticking your thumb into any guy's eye. Just a little.

Attr. Tony Galento (who floored Joe Louis briefly)

What we have here is the *Mona Lisa*. You want I should sell it like chicken liver?

Fight publicist Jerry Perenchio on Ali v. Frazier

Sports is a lot of damned nonsense.

Harry S. Truman

Games are silly but so are human beings.

Robert Lynd

Team spirit is an illusion you glimpse after you've won.

Steve Archibald, footballer, 1989

Show me a good loser in professional sports, and I'll show you an idiot.
Leo Durocher, baseball manager

We have a war to fight, too. The Washington Wizards are trying to make the play-offs. It's pretty much the same thing.
Basketball player Tyronn Lue, quoted in the *New York Times*, 2003, as the US invaded Iraq

So great was [Blackburn] Olympic's ambition to wrest the Cup from the holders that they introduced into football play a practice that has excited the greatest disapprobation in the south. For three weeks before the final they went into a strict course of training, spending, so report says, a considerable time at Blackpool and some days at Bournemouth and Richmond.
Eton College Chronicle, **3 May 1883 (FA Cup Final, 1883: Blackburn Olympic 2, Old Etonians 1)**

I always turn to the sports page first. The sports page records people's accomplishments; the front page nothing but man's failure.
Earl Warren, US Chief Justice

The secret of managing a club is keeping the five guys who hate you away from the five who are undecided.
Casey Stengel, baseball manager

JOHN MCENROE: I think I've improved as a person.
VOICE AT BACK OF PRESS CONFERENCE: There was plenty
   of room for improvement.
MCENROE: What did you say?
VOICE: I said there was plenty of room for improvement.
MCENROE: You're an asshole.
Scene at Wimbledon, 1985

The perfect balance for a team: seven roadsweepers and
four violinists.
Attr. Lawrie McMenemy, football manager

Formula One exists to sell tyres to the gullible, engines to
the affluent.
Patrick Collins, *Mail on Sunday*, 2004

A pressure game . . . When you look at a cheerleader and
don't notice her body.
Al McGuire, basketball coach

. . . when you play for five bucks with only two in your
pocket.
Lee Trevino, golfer

Pressure is a Messerschmitt up your arse.
Keith Miller, cricketer and wartime pilot

It's my bum in the bacon-slicer.
Mick McCarthy, football manager

If Wolves get relegated, they are going to give me an illuminated address: they'll burn my house down.
Tommy Docherty, football manager, 1984

Fulham Football Club Seek A Manager/Genius. Apply with CV to . . .
Advert, 1991

Being with a woman all night never hurt a professional baseball player. It's staying up all night looking for women that does him in.
Casey Stengel

I don't mind my players having sex before a game as long as I know they haven't enjoyed it.
Roy Masters, Australian rugby-league coach

Just for once, I'd like a player's fiancée to look like Olive from *On the Buses*.
John McKeown

INTERVIEWER (Gerry Williams): What do you think happened?
BORIS BECKER: Basically I lost a tennis match. I didn't lose a war. Nobody died.
Interview at Wimbledon, 1987

It is its want of variety that will prevent lawn tennis taking its rank among our great games . . . its monotony

compared with other sports will choke sportsmen off before they have time to excel in it.
Spencer Gore, first Wimbledon champion, 1877

I rang my cousin in India and mentioned my concern about England being knocked out. He told me how concerned he was about being knocked off the face of the earth by nuclear conflict.
Letter to the *Guardian*, during the 2002 soccer World Cup, from Arindam Raj of Hull

Dominoes . . . we think it will be the next cool thing.
Lino Garcia, ESPN spokesman, quoted in *The Times*, 2006

An amateur: a guy who won't take a cheque.
Paul Gallico

Bryn Jones signed for Arsenal for a record £14,000 in 1938. Bryn, very shy, was primed to ask: 'Can I have a little extra something?' George Allison, the manager, boomed out for his assistant to come in, then said: 'Repeat what you have just said to me and I'll have you drummed out of football. Now sign.' He did. 'And another thing. You can give up smoking.'
Ken Jones

Every golfer can expect to have four bad shots a round. When you do, just put them out of your mind . . .
Walter Hagen

. . . This, of course, is hard to do when you are still not off the first tee after you've had them.
Jim Murray

The most exquisitely satisfying act in the world of golf is that of throwing the club. The full backswing, the delayed wrist action, the flowing follow-through, followed by that unique whirring sound, reminiscent only of a passing flock of starlings, are without parallel in sport.
Henry Longhurst

Golf is a sport for white men dressed like black pimps.
Attr. Tiger Woods

The Thomson homer [that gave the New York Giants the 1951 National League pennant] continues to live because it happened decades ago when things were not replayed and worn out and run down before midnight on the first day. The scratchier an old film or an old audio tape, the clearer the action in a way. Because it's something that is preserved and unique.
Don DeLillo, *Underworld*

. . . And now the worst news of all. Gay men are getting interested in football. News of gay soccer (and rugby!) teams has started popping up in newspapers and magazines for homosexual readers. What a catastrophe.

One became a homosexual to get away from this sort of thing. If being gay does not give you a passport out of football-land, I begin to wonder what is the point of it.

Matthew Parris, *The Times*, 1998

Predictions

Pish! A woman might piss it out.

Sir Thomas Bloodworth, Lord Mayor of London, briefly awakened on the outbreak of the Great Fire, 1665

There never was a time when, from the situation, we might more reasonably expect fifteen years of peace.

William Pitt, 1792, just before the war with France

I fear that the development of railways will destroy the need for waterproof coats.

Attr. Charles Mackintosh

A flat failure.

Abraham Lincoln assessing the Gettysburg Address

The executive director of the American Association of Blacksmiths remarked that he had read about the automobile but that he was convinced it would have no consequence for the future of his organisation.

Neil Postman, *Amusing Ourselves to Death*

Forget it, Louis, no Civil War picture ever made a nickel.

Irving Thalberg advising Louis B. Mayer on *Gone With The Wind*

No Congress of the United States ever assembled, on surveying the state of the union, has met with a more pleasing prospect than that which appears at the present time.

President Coolidge's last State of the Union message, December 1928

When the Paris Exhibition closes, electric light will close with it, and no more be heard of.

Professor Erasmus Wilson, 1878

I doubt if type-setting by machinery will ever be as efficient or indispensable as hand-setting.

Ralph D. Blumenfeld, editor of the *Daily Express*, 1887

He [Tube-line builder Charles Yerkes] predicted to me that a generation hence London will be completely transformed, that people will think nothing of living twenty or more miles from town, owing to the electrified trains . . . I think he is a good deal of a dreamer.

Ralph D. Blumenfeld, 1900

These things represent a foolish waste of money. Besides, flying the Channel means nothing after you have done it. After all, you can't carry goods or passengers.

Ralph D. Blumenfeld, 1909

There's no market for talking pictures.

Edison

Get rid of that lunatic. He might have a knife.

Attr. Beverley Baxter, editor of the *Daily Express*, c. 1926, on being told a Mr John Logie Baird was in reception with an interesting invention

I shall take up dominoes again in my spare time.

Tsar Nicholas II, February 1917

I think there is a world market for maybe five computers.

Thomas Watson, Chairman of IBM, 1943

There is no reason why anybody would want a computer in their home.

Ken Olson, founder of Digital Equipment Corporation, 1977

In all likelihood, world inflation is over.

Per Jacobsson, Director of the IMF, 1959

Everything that can be invented has been invented.

Charles H. Duell, Commissioner, US Office of Patents, 1899

This 'telephone' has too many shortcomings to be seriously considered as a means of communication. This device is inherently of no value to us.

Western Union internal memo, 1876

No woman in my time will be Prime Minister or Foreign Secretary.

Margaret Thatcher, 1969

Race

*'I'm always rude to black bus conductors
in case they think I'm a patronizing white liberal.'*

In 1781 the British slaver *Zong* ran short of water in mid-Atlantic. 132 slaves were thrown into the sea on the reckoning that this way their loss would be covered by insurance, whilst their death from thirst would have thrown the loss on the owners.

Don Taylor, *The British in Africa*

'It's a free country, sir. The man's *mine*, and I do what I please with him – that's it.'
Harriet Beecher Stowe, *Uncle Tom's Cabin*

Was it barbarous to 'correct' a slave by putting him in the stocks, or by forcing him to wear chains or an iron collar? How severely might a slave be flogged before the punishment became brutal? These were matters of personal taste.
Kenneth M. Stampp, *The Peculiar Institution*

'That way,' he said, pointing. 'Follow the tree flowers,' he said. 'Only the tree flowers. As they go, you go. You will be where you want to be when they are gone.' So he raced from dogwood to blossoming peach. When they thinned out he headed for the cherry blossoms, then magnolia, chinaberry, pecan, walnut and prickly pear. At last he reached a field of apple trees whose flowers were just becoming tiny knots of fruit. Spring sauntered north, but he had to run like hell to keep it as his travelling companion.
Toni Morrison, *Beloved*

Passenger fares to the Morobe [the gold-mining area of New Guinea] will be £25 for Europeans. Natives will be charged as freight.
Announcement by Guinea Airways, 1920s, quoted in Anthony Sampson, *Empires of the Sky*

An indefensible society, and thus of course heavily defended: by regiments, naval squadrons, fierce dogs and Anglican clerics.

Joseph Hone on Barbados as a slave colony

The club system runs all through Barbadian life and the cold shoulder and the open snub are resorted to only when no legal quibble is available. It segregates the two races of islanders just as effectively as the most stringent colour discrimination in the United States and not half so honestly . . . It was without a pang that we flew away to Trinidad. Looking backwards we could almost see, suspended with the most delicate equipoise above the flat little island, the ghostly shapes of those twin orbs of the Empire, the cricket ball and the blackball.

Patrick Leigh Fermor, *The Traveller's Tree* (1950)

Part of this book was written while in South Africa in 1952. While there, salesmen approached me eager to offer me my choice of any new car for immediate delivery. We sat discussing the matter over a pleasant drink – which you can get at any time of day out there. There are no queues, no rations and income tax is relatively low. People seem to enjoy both work and play, and they still take a pride in work in that country. Their politicians may not always agree with ours in England but at least their people can trust them, and there is nothing like our National Health nonsense under which 'free' attention to a tooth costs £1. Cricketers love to get into a country enjoying these freedoms.

Walter Hammond, *Cricket's Secret History*

It seems that Andre Moritz had come across a play that had been popular on the other side of the sea; and he translated it into Afrikaans and adapted it to fit in with South African traditions. Andre Moritz's fault was that he hadn't adapted the play enough. The company made this discovery in the very first Free State *dorp* they got to. For when they left town, Andre Moritz had one of his eyes blackened, and not just with burnt cork. Andre Moritz adapted his play a great deal more, immediately after that. He made Uncle Tom into a much less kind-hearted Negro. And he also made him steal chickens. The only member of the company that the public of the backveld had any time for was the young man who acted Simon Legree.

Thus it came about that we heard of Andre Moritz's company when they were still far away, touring the Highveld, winding their play-actors' road northwards, past *koppies* and through *vlatkes*, and by blue-gums and willows. After a few more misunderstandings with the public, Andre Moritz so far adapted the play to South African conditions as to make Uncle Tom threaten to hit Topsy with a brandy bottle. The result was that by the time the company came to Zeerust, even the church elder, Thomas van Zyl, said there was much in the story of Uncle Tom that could be considered instructive.

H. C. Bosman, *Sold Down the River*

. . . the old dream of a country fit for farmers, where a man was free to ride his acres, father his children, lash his slaves, free from drought, English, Jews, missionaries, rinderpest, blacks, coolies and tax-collectors.

Christopher Hope, *Kruger's Alp*

Q: Is he being questioned?
SOUTH AFRICAN POLICEMAN: No, he's quite all right.

BBC interview, c. 1980

Q: Bishop Tutu says South Africa's sports fields are stained with the blood of the country's blacks.
WELSH RUGBY OFFICIAL: That's his problem, isn't it?

BBC interview at Johannesburg airport at the start of a tour, 1985

On Death Row [in South Africa], blacks get a white diet but on the last night a condemned white gets a chicken, a black only half a chicken.

Breyten Breytenbach, c. 1985

Once in New Orleans she slaked her thirst at a fountain in City Hall. 'All those people started *looking* at me. And me, so much a fool, I say to myself, "Oh, they know who I am,

I'm Mary Wells." Then I look up and see the sign. Yeah, you got it. WHITE ONLY. Me, in my little Motown star bubble. All of a sudden everything kind of crashes.'
Mary Wells, singer, quoted in her obituary, *Daily Telegraph*, 1992

They called me every name but a child of God.
Curt Flood, black baseball player, on playing in the Carolina League, c. 1956

From Afric's steaming Jungles
    To India's arid Plains
The Natives are dependent
    Upon the White Man's Brains

Instead of letting him exist
    Just how and where he pleases,
We teach him how to live like Us
    And die of Our Diseases.

We move him from his valleys
    To airy mountain-tops
Where he won't undermine his health
    By raising herds and crops.

The most disturbing nightmare
    Which haunts each White Man's son
Is 'If there had been no White Men
    What *would* the Blacks have done'.

Pont, *Lines*, c. 1935

Immigration is the sincerest form of flattery.
Attr. Jack Paar

It is undoubtedly true there is more unemployment among black people than among whites. I think we must give them a fair crack of the whip.
Norman Tebbit, quoted in *The Economist*, 1983

Like giving a child a latch-key, a bank account and a shotgun.
Herbert Morrison, British Foreign Secretary, on the idea of African independence, 1951

Bill Clinton's decision to site his office in the largely black Manhattan neighbourhood of Harlem, as a gesture of solidarity with African-Americans, appears to have backfired. Dozens of angry blacks demonstrated last week outside the building that houses the former president's staff, claiming that his move had led to the gentrification of the area and increased the prices of homes beyond their reach.
***Independent on Sunday*, 2006**

Really?

'What is it we're never supposed to do?'

All generalizations are dangerous, including this one.
Attr. Emerson

Ever since a great-aunt sent me a birthday card that said 'I was going to enclose some money, but I'd already sealed the envelope', I've been fascinated by paradoxes. Indeed, I've been collecting self-contradictory statements for decades now, from the classically simple ('I never tell the truth') to the ornately elegant ('Some people talk

about themselves in the third person, but you won't catch Victor Lewis-Smith doing that.')
Victor Lewis-Smith, *Evening Standard*, 2003

That would be absurd, seeing that I have but one.
Lord Nelson on a plan to rename a Yarmouth pub the Nelson Arms

Q: How would you like to be remembered?
ENOCH POWELL: I would like to have been killed in the war.
BBC interview, 1986

One said one fucking well wasn't going to do it, didn't one.
Overheard in the *Guardian* office, 1980

I stopped to pick a buttercup. Why people leave buttocks lying around I can't fathom.
Stephen Fry

They laughed when I said I was going to be a comedian. They're not laughing now.
Bob Monkhouse

All executives of the company are reminded that written authorisation is required for any proposed action of whatever nature. There is no exception to this rule.
Internal memo from Gerald Long, managing director of *The Times*, c. 1981

In the summer of 1988, Howard Marks 'apart from smoking over twenty joints a day' was 'super-straight and very settled'.
Guardian, 1996

A crossword clue says what it means but doesn't mean what it says.
Valerie Gilbert, crossword editor, *Daily Telegraph* 1996

'I saw the earth from the clouds.'
'Did it look round?'
'Yes, but I don't think it saw me.'
The Goons

Mention Merseyside and most people automatically think of the third-rail passenger system.
Rail magazine, 1998

Everyone knows that by 1400 the Christ Child in Western painting has shed Byzantine garb to appear more or less naked.
Guardian, 1984

If the person signing himself 'Homeless' will let us know his full name and address – not for publication – we will be pleased to give space to his letter.
Attr. *Evening Leader*, Wrexham, c. 1981

She asked for a double entendre so he gave her one.
Anon.

Lord Mowbray and Stourton: My Lords, can my noble
friend the Minister inform me whether or not this
Japanese knotweed is a cousin of our old friend sticky
willie, from which I suffer?
Hansard, 1989

ITIS APIS SPOTANDIS ABIGONE
**The inscription on a 'Roman vase' planted on an Essex newspaper by a
rival in the 1920s [Read the above carefully]**

We can't have people running around the beach
willy-nilly.
Councillor John Gray on regulating nudism in Brighton, 1989

Do you think the prisoners will regard you as a good
screw?
Jack de Manio, presenter of *Today*, to a female prison governor, c. 1965

I made him wear a condom but there must have been a
prick in it.
Attr. pregnant schoolgirl on *Kilroy*, c. 1990

Kingston council officer Martin Szalay was branded a
Satanist in the *News of* the *World*. He told the *Kingston
Informer*: 'This is a witch-hunt.'
***Press Gazette*, 1989**

The Farmington [Connecticut] Library Council, which
sponsored a 'TV turnoff' last January, decided this month
to proceed with a second effort . . . 'It will be interesting
to see if the impact is the same this year as last year,
when we had terrific media coverage,' Ellen Babcock said.
New York Times, 1984

Mr Scott, the churches should get together to stop all this
ecumenical nonsense.
Irishwoman to Nick Scott MP, *Observer*, 1986

What the man in the street is asking himself is: 'Why
does the government arbitrarily fix the rate of increase in
the money supply in the bracket between two particular
figures?'
Attr. Edward Heath

Sauna, massage, gymnastics: For these different services
you are kinkly requested to contact the reception desk in
advance.
Notice in Tunisian Hotel, 1982

'Lemme get this straight, Jim. Is it blind mother, deaf
     father, or the other way around?'
'How long have you been a black quarterback?'
'If you were a tree, what tree would you be?'
Questions asked of players at Superbowl press conferences, 1980s

One day, when I'm no longer about, I may have more to
say about what really happened in those days.
Sir Douglas Dodds-Parker, on the Special Operations Executive,
***The Times*, 2000**

I didn't know Henley was on the river.
Woman overheard in the Members' enclosure at the Royal Regatta,
1979

Hamilton Owens, one of [H. L. Mencken's] closest
associates . . . said of him: 'Never was a man more
gregarious, never one who strove more generously to
keep his friendships green.' In his diary Mencken called
Owens 'a time-server with no more principle in him
than a privy rat'.
Terry Teachout, *The Skeptic*

President Marcos of the Philippines went to New York
in September 1982 to address the UN General Assembly,
appealing for an early start to long-delayed negotiations
to bring about a more equitable distribution of wealth
between rich and poor nations. He arrived at the
Waldorf-Astoria with a delegation of a hundred, and
eight hundred suitcases, of which three hundred
belonged to his wife.
***Sydney Morning Herald*, 1983**

It is time for Arabs and Jews to sit down together and settle this matter in a true Christian spirit.

Senator Warren Austin, c. 1948

Religion

*'And now a prayer for those poor souls who
were damned for sins that are soft-pedalled now.'*

If we traverse the world it is possible to find cities
without walls, without letters, without kings, without
wealth, without coin, without schools and theatres,
but a city without a temple no one ever saw.
Petrarch

What is it the Bible [Old Testament] teaches us? Rapine, cruelty and murder. What is it the [New] Testament teaches us? To believe that the Almighty committed debauchery with a woman engaged to be married, and the belief of this debauchery is called faith.

Thomas Paine, *The Age of Reason*

In 1766 . . . the young Chevalier de la Barre failed to doff his hat in respect while a Capuchin religious procession passed through the streets of Abbeville. (It was raining.) He was charged and convicted of blasphemy, and sentenced to the torture 'ordinary and extraordinary', his hands to be cut off, his tongue torn out with pincers, and to be buried alive. This atrocious case haunted Voltaire for the rest of his life.

Paul Johnson, *A History of Christianity*

The English . . . prefer their religion as they used to like their clothing and cars, understated and reasonably reliable, there when you need it.

Jeremy Paxman, *The English*

'I know there's differences in religion. Some kinds is mis'rable. Ther's your meetin' pious; there's your singin', roarin' pious; them ar an't no account in black or white. But these rayly is; and I've seen it in niggers as often as any – your rail softly, quiet, stiddy, honest, pious, that the hull world couldn't tempt 'em to do nothin' that they thinks is wrong.'

Harriet Beecher Stowe, *Uncle Tom's Cabin*

'I've got a religion – my own religion,' the chemist answered, 'in fact, I've got more than the lot of them, with all their mumbo-jumbo – I worship God! I believe in the Supreme Being; a Creator, no matter who he be, who has placed us here below to do our duty as citizens and fathers. But I don't need to kiss a lot of silverplate in the church, and support a pack of humbugs who live better than we do ourselves! You can praise God just as well in the woods and the fields, or by gazing up into the vault of heaven, like the ancients . . . I cannot worship an old fogey of a God who walks round his garden with a stick in his hand, lodges his friends in the bellies of whales, dies with a cry on his lips and comes to life again three days later; all of which is intrinsically absurd and utterly opposed, moreover, to all physical laws.'

Gustave Flaubert, *Madame Bovary*

Do you know St Matthew mentions Hell 15 times in 52 pages of my Bible and St John not once? St Mark twice in 31 pages and St Luke three times in 52. Well, of course, St Matthew was a tax collector and believed in the efficacy of punishment, but it made me wonder.

Graham Greene, *Monsignor Quixote*

I have always found a Bible or a prayer book in a person's hand to be a sign of an uncharitable disposition.

W. H. Davies, _Autobiography of a Supertramp_

The Society for the Propagation of the Christian Gospel ran plantations in Barbados, and piously branded the word 'Society' on to the skin of each new slave.

Robert Winder, _Bloody Foreigners_

It was the very competitiveness of rival religions in the United States, acting by analogy to the free enterprise system, which kept the demands of the spiritual life consistently before the people.

Johnson, op. cit.

'Years ago I remember being very impressed by that Patrick Devlin, you remember the Devlin brothers they ran most of the Bronx beer at the time. So we was just getting started and I wanted to teach him a lesson, he was a tough one, we hung him up by the thumbs, you remember, Lulu? But he didn't know what we had in mind he thought we were killing him and he screamed for a priest. Well that impressed me. Not his mother, not his wife, not nobody but his priest when he thought he was dying. It gave me pause for thought. I mean you look to your strengths at a moment like that, am I right?'

E. L. Doctorow, _Billy Bathgate_

As God once said, and I think rightly . . .

Attr. Field Marshal Montgomery

Belief in the gospels . . . is confined to ecclesiastical reactionaries, pious old ladies and men about to be hanged.

H. L. Mencken, *The Philosophy of Friedrich Nietzsche*, 1907

After the Second Lateran Council, of 1139, priestly marriages were regarded as *a priori* invalid and all priests' wives as concubines; indeed, priests' children officially became the church's property as slaves. There was furious mass protest by the clergy, especially in northern Italy and Germany, but to no avail. Henceforth there was a universal and compulsory law of celibacy, though in practice up to the time of the Reformation this was observed only with qualifications, even in Rome.

Hans Küng, *The Catholic Church*

He [John Paul II] has always placed great store in apparitions of the Virgin, and has visited sites all over the globe – in Guadeloupe (the Black Madonna), Argentina (Virgin of the Apparition), the Philippines (Virgin of Perpetual Help), Lourdes and elsewhere . . . It has become commonplace to compare Karol Wojtyla, in the twilight of his reign, to Pius IX, the liberal cardinal who ascended to the papacy in 1846 at the young age of fifty-four. Disillusioned with liberalism after the experience of the

revolutions of 1848, he retreated into deep conservatism and promulgated the doctrine of the Immaculate Conception of the Blessed Mary in 1854 and the doctrine of Papal Infallibility at the Vatican Council of 1869–70. In his Syllabus of Errors of 1864, he listed eighty errors of modernity, the last of which reads 'that the Roman Pontiff can and should reconcile himself to and agree with progress, liberalism and modern civilization'.
New York Review of Books, 1996

There have been complaints about this priest before, and once I had to speak to his superior about him. It would seem that there has been no improvement. I shall speak to his superior again.
Letter from Cardinal Cahal Daly, Primate of All Ireland, to a paedophile priest's victim's family, *Guardian*, 1994

Everyone in the village calls the priest 'Father', except his sons, who call him 'Uncle'.
Irish saying

I know I am God because when I pray to Him I find I'm talking to myself.
Film: *The Ruling Class* (1972)

He is Father. Even more God is Mother, who does not want to harm us.
Pope John Paul I

And though she [my grandmother] never spoke of it, and no doubt seldom thought of it, she was a religious woman. That is to say she conceived of life as a road down which one travelled, an easy enough road through a broad country, and that one's destination was there from the very beginning, a measured distance away, standing in the ordinary light like some plain house where one went in and was greeted by respectable people and was shown to a room where everything one had ever lost or put aside was gathered together, waiting. She accepted the idea that at some time she and my grandfather would meet and take up their lives again, without the worry of money, in a milder climate. She hoped that he would somehow have acquired a little more stability and common sense.

Marylynne Robinson, *Housekeeping*

NED FLANDERS: Is God angry with me?
REVD LOVEJOY: The short answer is yes with an if. The long answer is no with a but.

The Simpsons

'Alec, what do you believe in? . . .'
'I believe an 11 bus will take me to Hammersmith. I don't believe it's driven by Father Christmas.'

John le Carré, *The Spy Who Came In From The Cold*

Theology is a trap that lies in wait for the lonely.

Evelyn Waugh

Je suis né chrétien, et je mourrai sans doute en cet état.
Dans l'intervalle . . .
François Mitterrand, President of France

It's all right to pray whilst eating sandwiches, but not all right to eat sandwiches whilst praying.
Rt Revd 'Mick' Mercier, Bishop of Exeter, quoted in his obituary, *The Times*, 2003

I never call on God for help when I'm in difficulties. If he dumps me in the drink, why should he come and fish me out again?
Eric Tabarly, yachtsman, quoted in the *Guardian*, 1997

The immortality of the soul: what a boring conception. I can't imagine anything worse than living for infinity in some great transcendental hotel with nothing to do in the evenings.
John Mortimer, *A Voyage Round My Father*

Q: Let's come to the misunderstandings. One of the most glaring errors you cite is that of the virgins promised, in the Islamic paradise, to the suicide bombers.
A: We begin from the term *huri*, for which the Arabic commentators could not find any meaning other than those heavenly virgins. But if one keeps in mind the derivations from Syro-Aramaic, that expression indicated 'white grapes', which is one of the symbolic

elements of the Christian paradise, recalled in the Last
Supper of Jesus . . .

Interview in *Süddeutsche Zeitung*, 2004, with 'Christoph Luxenberg',
pseudonym of a German professor who fears retaliation for writing
A Syro-Aramaic Reading of the Koran

. . . Imagine the disappointment!

Francis Wheen, *How Mumbo-Jumbo Changed the World*

HEREFORDSHIRE VICAR: And what do you do now?
EX-SAS MAN: I'm a mercenary.
VICAR: A missionary! How splendid!

Local anecdote

Science on the March

'I don't like the look of this.'

Fourteenth-century men seem to have regarded their doctor in rather the same way as twentieth-century men are apt to regard their priest, with tolerance for someone who was doing his best and the respect due to a man of learning but also with a nagging and uncomfortable conviction that he was largely irrelevant to the real and urgent problems of their lives.

Philip Ziegler, *The Black Death*

They [medieval doctors] were taught that illness sprang from an imbalance between the four humours (blood, phlegm, yellow bile and black bile) . . . Operations were largely confined to amputations, trepanning the skull, cutting for stone, bone-setting and incising abscesses.

Keith Thomas, *Religion and the Decline of Magic*

[During the plague] the Lord Mayor ordered the eradication of all dogs and cats, in the belief that they spread pestilence. Pepys reckoned 40,000 dogs and perhaps five times as many cats were killed (it must, alas, have been the perfect recipe for safeguarding the rats).

Roy Porter, *London: A Social History*

All knowledge that is not the real product of observation, or of consequences deduced from observation, is entirely groundless and illusory.

J.-B. Lamarck, French zoologist (1744–1829)

We have discovered the secret of life.

Francis Crick to James Watson in Cambridge pub after discovering DNA, 1953

The pulsar Vela, in the constellation Vega, is so dense that a fragment the size of a sugar cube would weigh 20,000 million tons.

***Daily Telegraph*, 1990**

When I heard the learn'd astronomer,
When the proofs, the figures, were ranged in columns
      before me,
When I was shown the charts and diagrams, to
      add, divide and measure them,
When I sitting heard the astronomer where he lectured
      with much applause in the lecture-room,
How soon unaccountable I became tired and sick
Till rising and gliding out I wander'd off by myself,
In the mystical moist night-air, and from time to time,
Look'd up in perfect silence at the stars.

Walt Whitman

. . . I can't think of anything more trivial than the speed of light. Quarks, quasars – big bangs, black holes – who gives a shit? . . . Is the universe expanding? Is it contracting? Is it standing on one leg singing 'When Father Painted the Parlour'? Leave me out. I can expand my universe without you. 'She walks in beauty, like the night of cloudless climes and starry skies, and all that's best of dark and bright meet in her aspect and her eyes.' There you are, he wrote it after coming home from a party.

Tom Stoppard, play: *Arcadia*

Bitter infusions of willow bark were anciently employed by country people as a remedy for chills, rheumatism and 'the ague' . . . The remedy worked, and early in the nineteenth century the active ingredient, salicylic acid, was isolated, both from willow bark and from meadowsweet (another plant of damp places). This led in 1899 to the synthesis of what was to become the world's most widely used – and useful – synthetic drug, acetylsalicylic acid, which the pharmaceutical company Bayer called aspirin, after the old botanical name for meadowsweet, *Spiraea ulmaria*.

Richard Mabey, *Flora Britannica*

A short history of medicine:

	'I have earache'
2000 BC	Here, eat this root.
AD 1000	That root is heathen. Here, say this prayer.
AD 1850	Prayer is superstition. Here, drink this potion.
AD 1940	That potion is snake oil. Here, swallow this pill.
AD 1985	That pill is ineffective. Here, take this antibiotic.
AD 2000	That antibiotic is artificial. Here, eat this root.

Anon.

Neanderthals had brains slightly larger than our own.

Jared Diamond, *Guns, Germs and Steel*

In my view, every drug packet should be marked: 'The safety and efficacy of this product were only made possible with animal tests.' The last big drug disaster in the UK happened because of a lack of animal research. Four decades ago, when thalidomide's awful effects were revealed, the drug was returned to the lab to be tested on pregnant animals for the first time. Birth defects were quickly seen in mice and rabbits. This prompted an overhaul of the legislation and is the basis for our laws on drug development. It is time my colleagues got real.

Robert Winston, *Guardian,* **2006**

Screenstruck

Good movies are unpredictable but logical.
Mediocre movies are predictable and logical.
Bad movies are predictable but illogical.
**Andrei Konchalovsky, Russian film-maker, quoted in the *Chicago
Tribune*, 1998**

Even trashy movies can make you cry.
Ian McEwan, *Enduring Love*

Just say two plus two. Let them say four.
Billy Wilder

We make movies, not films. We leave that to the French.
Sam Shepard, *True West*

The film is so cryptic as to be almost meaningless.
If there is any meaning it is doubtless objectionable.
**British Board of Film Censors banning *The Seashell and the Clergyman*,
1928**

We may take pride in observing that there is not a single
film showing in London today which deals with any of
the burning issues of the day.
Lord Tyrell, President, British Board of Film Censors, 1937

What is it about the movies? Stalin and Hitler loved them, all the major liars and tyrants seem to have been fans. They are beloved of all simplifiers, the purveyors of ideologies and alibis. Do they really exercise some gravitational impulse on life that flattens out character and extracts obviousness from the myriad chambers of reality? Is it their photographic dimension that makes them congenial to propaganda? Do pictures lie more readily than words?

Robert Stone, *New York Review of Books*, 1994

You can't go wrong with integrity. It's a good thing to admire. Bresson had so much of it that once, when trying to film the silence of some mournful wood, he sent men out with guns to shoot the jarringly cheerful birds.

Julian Barnes, *Metroland*

Cue the sun.

Film: *The Truman Show* (1998)

JOHN WAYNE, playing the Centurion in *The Greatest Story Ever Told*: 'Truly this was the Son of God.'

GEORGE STEVENS, director: 'I wonder, Mr Wayne, if you could say that line only with perhaps a little more awe.'

WAYNE: 'Aw, truly this was the Son of God.'

Anecdote

My face is the same and so is the dialogue. Only the horses have changed.

Audie Murphy on B-movie Westerns

I saw a specialist who asked me, 'Are you familiar with the phrase faecal impaction?' I said I think I saw that one with Glenn Close and Michael Douglas.

Bob Monkhouse

People don't go to the movies to be depressed. They go to the theatre for that.

Marie Jones, *Stones in His Pockets*

Five stages in the life of an actor:

1. Who is Mary Astor?
2. Get me Mary Astor.
3. Get me a Mary Astor type.
4. Get me a young Mary Astor.
5. Who is Mary Astor?

Mary Astor

Stagestruck

'Mother!! Father!! I've got into melodrama school!!!'

Having a pig costs more than twice the weekly wages of an actor.

David Edwards of the Derby Playhouse, quoted in the *Observer*, 1989

You are playing two dots at the moment, and I think if you check in the script you'll find it is three.

Harold Pinter to actor, quoted in the *Observer*, 1993

A theatre isn't a place where you can impose rules on people, it's a dirty radical place where an actor can work with a fag in his hand, a place where someone like me, or you if you felt the need, can piss down the staircase.

Sir Michael Gambon on attempts to ban smoking at the National Theatre, quoted in the *Guardian*, 2003

It is still forbidden in green rooms to name the play [the Scottish one] or quote from it, something you might do inadvertently, for instance by saying you had won 'golden opinions' from the reviewers. An offender is obliged to leave the room and, in a corridor, turn thrice in a circle and swear an oath. He or she may then be readmitted. Or if immediately on offending a culprit remembers to quote Hamlet's 'Angels and ministers of grace defend us!' he or she may stay in the room. The theatre is still a magical place, in part a leftover from a pre-scientific age, and all this is pure archaic magic, like the prohibitions on having fresh flowers on the stage, wearing green and whistling – a ban that also exists in the Navy. In fact one of my informants argued that in the old days stagehands were often ex-sailors whose superstition infected the players.

Frank Kermode, *New York Review of Books*, 1995

The theatre is an attack on mankind carried on by magic: to victimize an audience every night, to make them laugh and cry and suffer and miss their trains. Of course actors regard audiences as enemies, to be deceived, drugged, incarcerated, stupefied. This is partly because the audience is also a court against which there is no appeal. Art's relation with its client is here at its closest and most immediate. In other arts we can blame the client: he is stupid, unsophisticated, inattentive, dull. But theatre must, if need be, stoop – and stoop – until it attains that direct, that universal communication which other artists can afford to seek more deviously and at their ease.

Iris Murdoch, *The Sea, The Sea*

The blood-soaked living room is strewn with the body parts of Brendan and Joey, which Donny and Davey, blood-soaked also, hack away at to sizable chunks. Padraig is sitting on Christy's corpse, stroking Wee Thomas's headless dirt-soiled body. Through Christy's mouth, with the pointed end sticking out of the back of his neck, has been shoved the cross with 'Wee Thomas' on it.

Martin McDonagh, *The Lieutenant of Inishmore*, stage directions, Scene Nine

... I'd like to record for posterity the inspired gutting of my own review of *Sideways Glance*. The advert had the line 'Stylish, beautifully performed, this show is unmissable ...' Fair enough. My piece in the *Independent*

read: '. . . this show is unmissable for anyone who speaks Portuguese.'
Letter to *Time Out* from Alex Renton

I am convinced one of the chief pleasures of going to the theatre in Brighton is leaving it. The sleek Sussex matrons sit poised in the slips like greyhounds in the slips. The first 'fuck' and they're a mile down the front, streaking for Hove.
Alan Bennett

The *Stage* newspaper . . . I cannot quite bring myself to believe Kenneth Williams' sighting of an appeal for engagements by a dancer called Fanny ('Fun with a Frankfurter!') but in my rep days I always looked forward to the latest announcement from Kardomah who claimed to be able to 'fill the stage with flags' . . . My favourite was from the cricket fanatic Sir Frank Benson, who invited auditions for *Rosencrantz and Guildenstern* from actors who were 'handy in the gully'.
John Le Mesurier, *A Jobbing Actor*

According to legend, the Royal Shakespeare Company once posted a warning to audiences: 'This production contains real fire' . . . If the audience were indeed entitled to know about elements that might alarm, distress or offend them, why should this be restricted to effects?

No show is perfect, and shouldn't managements also alert the public to things they really have a right to know about, such as dicky casting, gloomy lighting or cheapskate design?

David Edgar, *Guardian*, 2006

No fancy salaries and no queer folk.

Advert for repertory actors, c. 1950

Television

There is an absolute ban upon the following: jokes about lavatories, effeminacy in men, immorality of any kind, suggestive references to honeymoon couples, chambermaids, fig leaves, ladies' underwear, lodgers and commercial travellers.

From the *BBC Green Book*, 1950s

You don't get any pornography on the telly. Get filth, that's all.

Johnny Speight, *Till Death Us Do Part*, 1972

Three-quarters of television is for half-wits. The boxing is all right.

Sir Thomas Beecham

Tell me, do you think television is here to stay?

Sir Keith Joseph, British politician, 1981

All she has to say is 'The mood here is one of cautious optimism' and flash her cleavage. A parrot with tits could do it.

Andy Hamilton and Guy Jenkin, *Drop the Dead Donkey*

Friends of mine recently returned from Britain tell me that one cannot see a programme which does not show

black and white living together, where they are not
continually propagating a mixture of the two races.
Albert Hertzog, South African Minister of Posts and Telegrams,
rejecting television, late 1960s. (It arrived in 1976.)

Television isn't something you watch, it's something you
appear on.
Quentin Crisp

One don who had criticised Alan [A. J. P. Taylor] for his
journalism was asked to appear on television for the first
time. The invitation specified the fee. 'Thank you for your
kind invitation, which I am delighted to accept,' replied
the don. 'I enclose a cheque for £35.'
Adam Sisman, *A. J. P. Taylor*

— My sister slept with my three husbands.
— I'm pregnant and have to strip.
— My teenager worships Satan.
— I stole my twelve-year-old's boyfriend.
— I married a horse.
Subjects on *The Jerry Springer Show*, quoted in the *Sunday Telegraph*,
2000

It is easy to occupy the moral high ground. What's more
difficult is to confidently occupy the moral low ground.
Jerry Springer – The Opera

Can you do anagrams? Imagine you are hanging from a beautiful silver star in the sky. Do you want an hour of news in depth? Are you sexually liberated, socially aware and politically concerned? Do you wear leg warmers? Have you read *An Ice-Cream War*? Do you believe in Veronyka Bodnarec and Victoria Poushka-Relf?

No? Then take your sticky hands off my nice new shiny channel.

Nancy Banks-Smith, *Guardian*, on the opening night of Channel 4, 1982

It is a fact that my children by the age of seventeen will have seen sixteen thousand people murdered on television and not one couple making love.

Anonymous parent, Channel 4, 1986

American television . . . a world in which the audience speaks to the artist instead of the other way round.

Ralph Schoenstein, quoted in the *Observer*, 1984

Television news directors across the US seek broadcasters who speak 'Iowan', that is, with nary an accent.

Stephen G. Bloom, *Postville*

You think I'm crazy? Who wants to look at that? It's too downbeat. The girl's got a limp.

Jim Aubrey, President of CBS, declining to show *The Glass Menagerie*

TV executives would want to rewrite *Gone With The Wind*. If they had *The Old Man and the Sea*, they'd say to the author: 'Ernie, we love it. But the part about the fish is boring. And the man is too old. He should have a girlfriend.'
Jim Bouton

. . . Andrew Cunanan [wanted for murdering Gianni Versace], may have been motivated by revenge because he has the AIDS virus. Also he may be cross-dressing to evade capture. We have a report. Plus a guest thinks we may be turning him into a celebrity.
NBC Today, 1997

We seemed to have a lot of brain tumours over the years.
Actress Jane Rossington reminiscing on the end of *Crossroads* in the
TV Times, 1988

The Thatcher Years

'Tell me, that time back in May 1982 – did you really believe Scargill was on board the Belgrano?'

Bryan McAllister

It is exciting to have a real crisis on your hands when you have spent half your political life dealing with humdrum issues like the environment.
Thatcher to the Scottish Conservative Conference during the Falklands War, 1982

The Perez de Cuellar [UN secretary-general] peace plan was doomed. Mummy could never take him seriously because Daddy kept calling him Pina Colada.
Attr. Carol Thatcher

You got to sock a picket or two.
Graffito

Well, there's more to nick.
Douglas Hurd, Home Secretary, explaining the rising crime rate, 1987

One change that has come over public manners was evident at the Falklands homecomings. Combatants (the only airman captured by the Argentinians, for instance), asked what is the first thing they are going to do when they get home, grin cheekily. One says, 'Well, what do you think?' and doubtless others actually do say, 'I'm going to fuck someone silly.' Once upon a time they would have *said*, at any rate, 'Have a nice cup of tea.'
Alan Bennett, *Diaries*, 1982

The only other contribution that I felt I could make was to do my bit towards the 'six o'clock surge'. This was an underground plan that was relayed to me by some bearded lefty I had listened to at a party as he sat on a bean bag taking far too long to roll a joint. He told me that the media were suppressing news of an effective campaign by socialists everywhere, a scam which was rapidly exhausting the government's huge reserves of coal. The idea was to suddenly increase the demand for electricity at a given point in the day because a huge surge apparently made far greater demands on the power stations than generally increased consumption.

Every day thereafter I ran around the house at six o'clock in the evening turning on kettles, immersion heaters, steam irons, electric fires, hair-dryers and the yoghurt-maker in the hope that the resultant draining of electricity would bring power cuts and the collapse of the Thatcher government within a couple of weeks. The campaign lasted right up until the arrival of the next electricity bill when I realized I had almost bankrupted us.

John O'Farrell, *Things Can Only Get Better*

I think, basically, she's hijacked the Tory Party from the landowners and given it to the estate agents.

Denis Healey, 1987

During the high months of his [Health Minister John Moore] status as her chosen successor he framed the NHS reforms exactly on the basis of what he thought she wanted. But she kept changing her mind. One minute she wanted him to go further, the next she got an attack of the doubts, wanted him to trim a bit. Each time he agreed, made the adjustments, came back for approval. The result was a total hotchpotch and she ended up thinking he was a wanker and got rid of him.

Alan Clark, *Diaries*

She's gone through hospital wards like a latter-day
Florence Nightingale – with a blow-lamp.
Denis Healey, 1989

When she's finally laid to rest, they will find Dunroamin
engraved on her heart.
Keith Waterhouse

Britain after Thatcher . . . like *Crossroads* after Noele
Gordon left.
Mark Steyn, *Evening Standard*, 1991

When I want an image of what Mrs Thatcher has done
to Britain I think of the carol singers. At the time she
came to power, they would, as they always had, sing a
carol or two, then ring the bell and, if you answered, sing
some more. Halfway through the rule of Thatch, I began
noticing that they wouldn't bother to start singing until
they had first rung the bell and checked that you were
there to listen and pay up. After she had been in power
for about ten years, I opened the door one Christmas and
peered out. There were two small boys some distance
from the house already, unwilling to waste their time if
they got a negative response. 'Carols?' one of them asked,
spreading his hands in a business-like gesture, as if he
had just acquired a job lot of tunes off the back of a lorry
and could perhaps be persuaded to cut me in.
Julian Barnes, *New Yorker*, 1993

How prosperous, how influential, how they had flourished under a government they had despised for almost seventeen years. Talking 'bout my generation. Such energy, such luck. Nurtured in the post-war settlement with the State's own milk and juice, and then sustained by their parents' tentative, innocent prosperity, to come of age in full employment, new universities, bright paperback books, the Augustan age of rock and roll, affordable ideals. When the ladder crumbled behind them, when the State withdrew her tit and became a scold, they were already safe, or they consolidated, and settled down to forming this or that – taste, opinions, fortunes.

Ian McEwan, *Amsterdam*

Travellers' tales

'That's funny – it says here that Tuesday is Market Day.'

In my opinion it's a very second-class place. It doesn't compare with Portsmouth . . . I shall never come abroad again.

Admiral Sir John Fisher, writing to his wife from Geneva

Mr Eustace, the classical tourist, did not think much of it [Venice]; . . . he compared the Rialto, greatly to its disadvantage, with Westminster and Blackfriars Bridges.
Charles Dickens, *Little Dorrit*

Rhodesia: Surrey with the lunatic fringe on top.
Anon.

Pyongyang's subway is the prettiest and most poetic mass-transit system in the world. Escalators of astonishing length angle into the earth through Cyclopean tunnels, their walls pristinely white. The station platforms are like the stage sets from a nineteenth-century opera, with murals depicting the river banks of Pyongyang in their spring glory.
Richard Lloyd Parry, *The Times*, **2004**

It used to be said of the colonnaded verandah of the Continental Palace Hotel in Saigon that it was hardly ever necessary to leave it. To demonstrate to a doubting newcomer how life could be conducted without budging from the 'Continental Shelf', a long-time resident is supposed to have summoned a waiter. 'A citron soda for me; my friend would like a virgin, nothing too old, and a French passport.' The unauthorised version of the yarn is the waiter returning with the drink and the news that 'the virgin is on her way but the passport is difficult, about half an hour'.
Rowlinson Carter, *Spectator*, **1986**

My whole life, every white man's life in the east, was one long struggle not to be laughed at.

George Orwell, *Shooting an Elephant*

Taxi drivers in Frankfurt are said to dislike the annual Book Fair because literary folk, instead of being shuttled to prostitutes like respectable members of other convening professions, prefer to stay in their hotels and fuck one another.

Julian Barnes, *Cross Channel*

Bangui . . . the only place in the world where I have seen almost the entire French community drunk at ten o'clock in the morning – they drank white wine with their breakfast or, more often, instead of it.

Negley Farson, *Behind God's Back*, **1940**

He is a teetotaller, which is an untrustworthy habit among one's friends but not among one's African butler friends.

Hilary Hook, African hunter, *Home from the Hill*, **1987**

Kim Philby [in Moscow] kept homesickness at bay with regular supplies of marmalade, Pimm's No. 1, lime pickle and Gitanes, according to his widow Rufina.

Daily Telegraph, **1997**

Sending telegram, 'Leaving Friday', I had written 'Hoping foregather with you weekend'. The clerk, a sombre youth with steel-rimmed glasses, demurred at the word 'foregather'.

'Is not being proper English word.'

'Oh, but yes.'

'Is not being proper English word. No good.'

'I assure you it is a proper English word with a specific meaning. It means . . . '

'I am telling you.'

Weak as I was with heat and frustration, I felt this was a compelling challenge.

'I *know* this is a proper English word. Please send telegram.'

The clerk put a small sweetmeat into his mouth, climbed slowly from his tall stool and sauntered into the back shadows. After a decent interval, he returned, climbed with leisure back into his seat, and pushed my message to one side. He showed neither rancour nor triumph.

'Babu says not being proper English word. Next person, please.'

The crowd surged happily forward, the debate was clearly over. I wondered in a desultory way how my message had been sub-edited, in what shape it would turn up in Delhi. I need not have worried: naturally it never turned up at all.

James Cameron, *An Indian Summer*

The whole area, thousands of square miles, is simply untamed tropical fen; 'new mud, old mud and marsh', as a geographer has called it. The only firm ground is by the river banks, so that villages straggle along the watercourses, surrounded by mangoes, palms, bamboos and endless expanses of swamp. When the rains come and the rivers flood, this delta becomes a gigantic inland sea. At any time, it is a perfect breeding ground for malaria and any other disease that thrives on moisture . . . Yet on this bog the British created their capital in India. Nothing but commercial greed could possibly have led to such an idiotic decision.

Geoffrey Moorhouse, *Calcutta*

The most exciting way of getting into Russia is to cross Germany in a sealed train and arrive in the Finland Station in St Petersburg to be greeted by a cheering revolutionary mob who promptly rename the city after you. This approach being no longer possible, the next best method is to book a Sovereign package tour through British Airways.

Clive James, *Observer,* **c. 1987**

Ordinary courtesies in Arabic take on a quality of Miltonic grandeur when translated directly into English. Most of the people I had met either spoke English so well that they had absorbed an Anglo-American casualness along with the language, or their English was so broken that they could not find the heroic phrases they would have liked to use. Major Burza was unusual in that he spoke English with great fluency, but the content of what he said was almost exclusively Arabic. It was a little like trying to hold a conversation with Tristan or Don Giovanni.

Jonathan Raban, *Arabia*

In 1935 Addis Ababa had two places of entertainment: Le Select and the Perroquet. 'Both prospered on the contrast, because, after an hour in either place, one longed for the other.'

Evelyn Waugh, quoted in the *Financial Times*, **1998**

Theodore Monod had once described Tombouctou to me as 'a dreadful place', but in the time I spent there I could not see why . . . it was more colourfully of the desert than any place I had visited, with the billowing robes of the camel men running through a whole spectrum of shades that included deep royal blues, lime and avocado greens, gorgeous oranges and yellows.

Geoffrey Moorhouse, *The Fearful Void*

It did me good to go south, the better to see the north.

Vincent Van Gogh

No one in the world is so unintelligent as a single Japanese and no one so bright as two.

John Gunter, *Inside Asia* (1939)

The letters about travelling on Indian railways . . . brought to mind the following story told to me by a friend. The train for his destination duly arrived, but when he got on he found his seat, which he had reserved, was occupied by a Sikh gentleman. My friend checked the carriage and seat number and found them to be correct and so asked the man to move. He showed him his reservation, with the carriage and seat written on it, saying: 'Surely you must agree you are sitting in my place?' 'It is true that I am sitting in that seat,' said the man, 'but this is yesterday's train.'

Letter to the *Independent* from Peter Crawley, 1989

The New York socialite Sandy Hill Pittman, then wife of the co-founder of MTV, had her porters carry up the sacred slope [Everest] two laptops, five cameras, a CD player and an espresso machine, while other Sherpa runners brought her the latest editions of *Vanity Fair* and *Vogue*.

***New York Review of Books*, 1999**

São Paolo is just like Reading, only further away.

Peter Fleming, c. 1930

The Ixodes tick, which carries encephalitis, could kill or cripple you for life . . . Up to midsummer Russians only walk the taiga dressed in double layers of clothing.

Colin Thubron, *In Siberia*

THE *BOMBAY SAMACHAR*:
The 46th Oldest Newspaper In The World

NOGI'S MONKEY BRAND BLACK TOOTH POWDER

Summertime and the feeling is
. . . GRASIM GWALIOR SUITING

We are pleased to inform you
that we have specious bungalows

SEX AND THE ANIMALS IN WILD SPLENDOUR
(The Cameras Do Not Stop During The Mating Scenes)

Apply for a telephone now
– you may need it 5 years hence

Before you defecate make sure there is no latrine around

Signs spotted in India, c. 1985

. . . For most of the past fifty years, this fertile plain,
ringed by snow-capped mountains and home to a
rich mix of ethnic communities, was designated as
Zhongdian, a county in the Diqing Tibetan autonomous
prefecture of north-west Yunnan prefecture. That title
was never likely to attract visitors. So after the Cultural
Revolution, local officials lobbied the central government
to change the name. They faced stiff competition from
other Himalayan regions, which also claimed to be the
source of inspiration for James Hilton's novel, *Shangri-la*.

The ensuing contest to be the official utopia lasted the better part of a decade, until the state council announced in 2001 that Xiang-ge-ri-la – the Mandarin rendition of Shangri-la – was to be marked on all maps in the place previously occupied by Zhongdian. Now that paradise has been found, it has been overrun. In the year before the name-change, Shangri-la received 20,000 visitors. Last year, the number surged to 2.6 million.

Jonathan Watts, *Guardian*, 2006

Since Starbucks first ventured into China six years ago, it has opened 230 branches across the country, and plans to open a further 10,000 outlets over the next few years. 'It traditionally has been a tea-drinking country, but we turned them into coffee drinkers,' Howard Schultz, the chairman of Starbucks, said of China earlier this year. Although coffee's bitter tang is an alien taste on the tongues of the tea-drinking nation, the burgeoning middle classes see coffee – which, at the equivalent of £2 a cup, costs as much as the daily wages of an unskilled labourer – as an essential status symbol. 'People start drinking coffee because they think it's the cool thing to do,' said Serena Lee, a twenty-three-year-old manager of an English-language school. 'It's a statement. They feel sophisticated. Everyone is afraid of looking like a farmer.' Zhang Hui, twenty-eight, a computer analyst, who was strolling out of a café with a steaming paper cup in one hand and a Louis Vuitton handbag swinging by her side, said: 'A few years ago when I tasted coffee first, I thought it was disgusting. I never wanted to drink it again, but my boyfriend told me I would look backward if I refused to drink it. Later I got hooked. I don't know if I really like it, but sometimes I just need it.'

Peter Goff, *Sunday Telegraph*, 2006

HARARE – How bad is inflation in Zimbabwe? Well, consider this: at a supermarket near the centre of this tatterdemalion capital, toilet paper costs $417. No, not per roll. 417 Zimbabwean dollars is the value of a single two-ply sheet. A roll costs $145,750 – in American currency, about 69 cents. The price of toilet paper, like everything else here, soars almost daily, spawning jokes about a better use for Zimbabwe's $500 bill, now the smallest in circulation.

Michael Wines, *New York Times*, 2006

T-shirts

Collected by Bob Levey, *Washington Post* columnist, 2002

I'M DRESSED AND OUT OF BED
– WHAT MORE DO YOU WANT?

YOU'RE JUST JEALOUS BECAUSE
THE LITTLE VOICES ARE TALKING TO *ME*

FEED ME HORS D'OEUVRE AND I ANALYSE POLICY

I LIVE IN MY OWN WORLD BUT IT'S OK
– THEY KNOW ME HERE

. . . AND YOU SAY PSYCHO LIKE IT WAS A BAD THING

I HEAR VOICES – AND THEY DON'T LIKE YOU

I HAVE THE BODY OF A GOD
– UNFORTUNATELY THE GOD IS BUDDHA

WHAT PART OF ELEEMOSYNARY RATIOCINATION
DO YOU NOT UNDERSTAND?

GOT RID OF THE KIDS, THE CAT WAS ALLERGIC

HOW LONG A MINUTE IS DEPENDS ON
WHICH SIDE OF THE BATHROOM DOOR YOU'RE ON

WHERE ARE WE GOING?
WHY AM I IN THIS HANDBASKET?

DUE TO BUDGET CUTS,
THE LIGHT AT THE END OF THE TUNNEL
HAS BEEN CUT OFF

I MARRIED MR. RIGHT,
BUT I DIDN'T KNOW HIS FIRST NAME
WAS ALWAYS

I KNOW ABOUT STRESSED
– IT'S DESSERTS SPELLED BACKWARDS

The Upper Crust

What eye has wept for him? What heart has heaved a
throb of unmercenary sorrow? If he ever had a friend,
we protest that the name of him or her has not yet
reached us.

Obituary of George IV, *The Times*, 1830

Now, dear, where did you say you were king of?

**BBC receptionist to King Haakon of Norway during the
Second World War**

'Are you the fat activist?'
'I am Queen Anne-Marie of Greece.'

Reported exchange in Sky News green room, 1994

CHAPTER 20: INTERCOURSE WITH ROYALTY

Mrs Massey Lyon, *Etiquette; a guide to public and social life*, 1927

It took me some time to realize that this was not
first-class (!) although it puzzled me as to why the seat
seemed so uncomfortable. Such is the end of Empire,
I sighed to myself.

**Prince Charles, relegated to business class by the hordes of politicians,
en route to the Hong Kong handover, 1997**

Charles Philip Arthur George has the same initials as
the Child Poverty Action Group.
Guardian, 2000

Even his name was sacred: a man in faraway Hokkaido
called his child Hirohito, then found the Emperor was so
named, and killed both himself and the child. Death was
too good for anyone who transgressed in the imperial
presence: a policeman who misdirected the Imperial
motorcade, and sent it down an alley, slit his bowels open
once he realised his mistake.

The men who polished the imperial train had their
nails filed to the quick lest they scratch the black
lacquerwork. Doctors who examined the Imperial chest
and stomach were ordered to wear thin silk gloves. The
tailor who measured Hirohito for his suits had to do so
from a respectful distance (which accounts, some say, for
his Imperial Highness's execrable appearance in Western
clothes, and not much better in a kimono).
Simon Winchester, *Guardian*, 1987

Klaus Vogel, 36-year-old son of Frau Ilse van der Trenk
of Württemberg, is 4,363rd in line to the British throne
as the most distant known legitimate descendant of
George I.
Daily Mail, 2000

They need not be sound either in body or mind. They only
require a certificate of birth, just to prove they were first

of the litter. You would not choose a spaniel on those principles.
Lloyd George on the House of Lords, 1909

When I want a peerage, I shall buy one like an honest man.
Alfred Harmsworth, later Lord Northcliffe

On June 23 1894 . . . a mining disaster at Cilfynydd [near Pontypool] killed no less than 260 workers. The next day, the French President, M. Carnot, was assassinated. On the 25th, Sir William Harcourt, on behalf of the Government, moved that condolences should be sent to France over the last event. Keir Hardie rose to ask whether some official regrets should also be sent to those bereaved by the Cilfynydd disaster. 'Oh no,' replied Sir William airily, 'I can dispose of that now by saying the House does sympathise with these poor people.'
G. D. H. Cole and Raymond Postgate, *The Common People*

The dividing line between the House of Lords and Pentonville Jail is very thin.
Film: *O Lucky Man!* (1973)

Anyone who has been to an English public school will always feel comparatively at home in prison. It is people brought up in the gay intimacy of the slums . . . who find prison so soul-destroying.
Evelyn Waugh, *Decline and Fall*

Look, I want no formality on this trip. You may call me Sir.
Attr. the Duke of Norfolk, manager of the MCC tour of Australia 1962–63, to reporters

There are seventeen ways to address an air vice-marshal.
Sir Raymond Monbiot, Chairman of the Conservative Party board, explaining why it took so long to conduct leadership elections, 2005

When Lord Cowdray asked Lord Poole [the Chairman of Lazards] how he avoided lending money to all the financiers who failed in 1974, he replied: 'Quite simple, I only lent money to people who had been at Eton.'
Anthony Sampson, *The Changing Anatomy of Britain*

When you sign up online for Skywards, which is the frequent-flier program of Emirates, the international airline of the United Arab Emirates, you enter your name, address, passport number, and other information, and you select an honorific for yourself from a drop-down list. A few of the choices, in addition to the standard Mr, Mrs, Ms, Miss, and Dr, are: Admiral, Air Comm, Air Marshal, Al-Haj (denoting a Muslim who has made a pilgrimage to Mecca), Archbishop, Archdeacon, Baron, Baroness, Colonel, Commander, Corporal, Count, Countess, Dame, Deacon, Deaconess, Deshamanya (a title conferred on eminent Sri Lankans), Dowager (for a British widow whose social status derives from that of her late husband, properly used in combination with a second honorific, such as Duchess), Duchess, Duke, Earl, Father, Frau, General, Governor, HRH, Hon, Hon Lady, Hon Professor, JP (justice of the peace?), Judge, Khun (the Thai all-purpose honorific, used for both men and women), L Cpl, Lt, Lt Cmdr, Lt Col, Lt Gen, Midshipman, Mlle, Monsieur, Monsignor, Mother, Pastor, Petty Officer, Professor, Señor, Señora, Señorita, Sgt, Sgt Mjr, Shaikha (for a female shaikh, or sheikh), Sheikh, Shriman (an Indian honorific, for one blessed by Lakshmi, the Hindu goddess of wealth, wisdom, luck, and other good things), Sister, Sqdn Ldr, Sqn Ldr, Sub Lt, Sultan, Swami, The Countess, The Dowager, The Duchess, The Marquis, The Matron, The Revd Canon, the Reverend, The Rt Hon, The Ven, The Very Revd, Ven, Ven Dr, Very Revd, Vice Admiral, Viscount, and Viscountess.

David Owen, *New Yorker*, **2006**

Bourgeois and, what is more, provincial bourgeois!

Zola to the writer Barbey d'Avrevilly

Mr Speaker Hylton-Foster (d. 1965) dropped dead in Duke Street, the only street, someone said at the time, in which he would have wished to be seen dead.

Ian Aitken, *Guardian*, **1986**

I hope it doesn't take up too much time. I hunt four days a week.

Attr. Lord Halifax, on being appointed Foreign Secretary

The children of the Dukes of Somerset were not allowed to hunt more than three days a week until they were five years old . . . If they hunted six days a week it was feared it would spoil them.

Caroline Blackwood, *In the Pink*

My own wife, as some people know, had a lot of children. Eight, if I remember rightly.

Lord Longford, *Observer*, 1985

SIR ALEC GUINNESS: What do you do at home in the Borders?

LADY HOME: Good heavens! I do what every woman in the British Isles does, I spend the morning making sandwiches and then take them down to the men in the butts.

Exchange reported in *The Times*, 1996

John Clotworthy Talbot Whyte-Melville Skeffington, 13th Viscount Massereene and 6th Viscount Ferrard, 'Lord Mass of Cream and Feathers', observed during a debate on the Brixton riots that he thought he was 'the only member who has spoken today who has had agricultural estates in Jamaica'.

***Daily Telegraph*, 1992**

In the circles in which I move, sleeping with a woman does not constitute an introduction.

Attr. Lady Veronica McLeod, society beauty c. 1890, to a ship's steward the morning after an on-board liaison

INTERVIEWER: Do you think the class barriers have broken down?

BARBARA CARTLAND: Of course they have. Or I wouldn't be sitting here talking to someone like you.

Quoted in *The Times*, 1996

War

In the last 3,421 years of recorded history only 268 have seen no war.

Will and Ariel Durant, *The Lessons of History*, 1968

There's only one way for a young man to get on in the army. He must try to get killed in every possible way he can.

Sir Garnet Wolseley

'Certainly, my home at my uncle's brought me acquainted with a circle of admirals. Of *Rears* and *Vices* I saw enough. Now do not be suspecting me of a pun, I entreat.'

Jane Austen, *Mansfield Park*

The [US] Civil War was fought in 10,000 places . . . more than three million Americans fought in it and over 600,000 men, two per cent of the population, died in it. At Cold Harbor some 7,000 Americans fell in twenty minutes . . . Four of Lincoln's own brothers-in-law fought on the Confederate side, and one was killed. The little town of Winchester, Virginia changed hands seventy-two times during the war, and the state of Missouri sent thirty-nine regiments to fight in the siege of Vicksburg, seventeen to the Confederacy and twenty-two to the Union.

Geoffrey C. Ward, *The Civil War*

Photography had come of age just as the war began, and more than a million photographs of it are thought to have been made. While the fighting went on, the public appetite for the pictures was insatiable, but when it stopped no one seemed to want them any more, as if their vivid reality too painfully perpetuated in the mind the calamity just ended. Thousands of glass plates were sold to gardeners, not for the precious images they held, but for the glass itself. In the years following Appomattox, the sun slowly burned away the war from thousands of greenhouse panes.

ibid.

Warriors of the Zulu Army were compulsorily celibate until they had killed or wounded an enemy, which made for warlike men and sanguinary women.

Jan Morris, *Heaven's Command*

It will be a sad day when England has officers who know too well what they are doing. It smacks of murder.

Film: Lord Raglan in *The Charge of the Light Brigade* (1968)

In three and a half hours on the second day of the Battle of Loos, 1915, among twelve battalions totalling less than

10,000, the British casualties were 385 officers and 7,861 men. The Germans suffered no casualties at all.

Alan Clark, *The Donkeys*

The pinnacles of [German] atrocity were reached with the burning of Louvain, whose famous library contained a unique collection of mediaeval manuscripts, and the destruction of Dinant, where 678 civilians were massacred, including a child three weeks old. Not since the Thirty Years War had Europe known the meaning of such deliberate terror.

John Terraine, *The Great War*

Price was reading the roll call . . . He hurried from one unanswered name to the next. Byrne, Hunt, Jones, Tipper, Wood, Leslie, Barnes, Studd, Richardson, Savile, Thompson, Hodgson, Birkenshaw, Llewellyn, Francis, Arkwright, Duncan, Shea, Simons, Anderson, Blum, Fairbrother. Names came pattering into the dusk, bodying out the places of their forebears, the villages and towns where the telegram would be delivered, the houses where the blinds would be drawn, where low moans would come in the afternoon behind closed doors; and the places that had borne them, which would be like nunneries, like dead towns without their life or purpose, without the sound of fathers and their children, without young men at the factories or in the fields, with no husbands for the women, no deep sound of voices in the inns, with the children who would have been born, who would have grown and worked or painted, even governed, left ungenerated in their fathers' shattered flesh that lay in stinking shellholes in the beet-crop soil . . .

Sebastian Faulks, *Birdsong*

Now, tell me, was it you or your brother that was killed in the war?

Attr. Headmaster of Shrewsbury School to an old boy, 1919

Great Britain provided time, the United States provided money and Soviet Russia provided blood.

Stalin on the Second World War

During the retreat from Moscow, German soldiers seized any livestock and food supplies on which they could lay their hands. They ripped up floorboards in living rooms to check for potatoes stored underneath. Furniture and parts of houses were used for firewood. Never did a population suffer so much from both sides in a war. Stalin had signed an order on 17 November [1941] ordering Red Army units to 'destroy and burn to ashes' all houses and farms for up to 40 miles behind the German lines to deny the enemy shelter. The fate of Russian women and children was not considered for a moment.

Anthony Beevor, *Stalingrad*

About ten minutes of blind terror and five and a half
years of utter boredom.

My father, Flight-Lieutenant Max Engel (1912–2005), on his Second
World War

We had been flying all day long at one hundred
        fucking feet.
The weather fucking awful, fucking rain and
        fucking sleet;
The compass it was swinging fucking south and
        fucking north,
But we made a fucking landfall in the Firth of
        fucking Forth.
    (*Chorus*)
Ain't the air force fucking awful?
Ain't the air force fucking awful?
Ain't the air force fucking awful?
We made a fucking landing in the Firth of
        fucking Forth.

Anon., 'The Twats in the Ops Room', c. 1940

What was it about the war that moved the troops to
constant verbal subversion and contempt? It was not just
the danger and fear, the boredom and uncertainty and
loneliness and deprivation. It was rather the conviction
that optimistic publicity and euphemism had rendered
their experience so falsely that it would never be readily
communicable. They knew that in its representation to

the laity what was happening to them was systematically sanitized and Norman Rockwellized, not to mention Disneyfied. They knew that despite the advertising and publicity, where it counted their arms and equipment were worse than the Germans'.

Paul Fussell, *Wartime*

KEITEL (Hitler's Chief of Staff): What shall we do?
FIELD MARSHAL VON RUNDSTEDT: Make peace, you fools.

Reported exchange, July 1944

The war has developed, not necessarily to Japan's advantage.

Emperor Hirohito's surrender broadcast, 1945

[On VE Night] a South African air ace, Lt Col Pierce Joubert DSO, who had fought in the skies over Normandy and Arnhem and had led one of the first squadrons to take paratroops over the Rhine in March, was killed by a home-made firework he had constructed from a Verey light and an iron tube.

Robert Kee, *The World We Fought For*

A Sandhurst instructor in the 1950s used to tell officer candidates ... Never march on Moscow, never invade the Balkans and never trust personal luggage to the RAF.

***Daily Telegraph*, 1997**

Does anyone remember the Big Mac theory of combat prevention? The idea, propounded by the American journalist Thomas Friedman in his book *The Lexus and the Olive Tree*, was that there had never been a war between two countries which both had branches of McDonald's in their capital cities . . . Alas, by the time Friedman's book appeared in Britain last summer the US Air Force was already bombing Belgrade, even though there were seven McDonald's restaurants in the Serb capital.

Francis Wheen, *Guardian*, 2000

Almost fifty years ago now I felt compelled to write in a speech for Judge Danforth in *The Crucible*: 'You must understand, sir, a person is either with this court or he must be counted against it, there be no road between. This is a sharp time, now, a precise time – we live no longer in the dusky afternoon when evil mixed itself with good and befuddled the world. Now, by God's grace, the shining sun is up, and them that fear not light will surely praise it. I hope you will be one of those.'

How many times do we have to indulge the same idiocies for which we must later be ashamed?

Arthur Miller, *New York Times*, on the Iraq invasion, March 2003

Iraq has already achieved victory – apart from some technicalities.

Mohsen Khalil, Saddam's Ambassador to the Arab League, quoted in the *Washington Post*, April 2003

I do sympathize with Bush and Blair trying to find WMDs. I'm like that with my scissors. I put them down, then I search all over the house, and I never find them. Of course, I do know my scissors exist.
Linda Smith, Radio 4

This is propaganda. I was born and grew up in a propaganda country, and so I know it well. Actually, they do the propaganda very well, better than we do it. We in China can learn from this propaganda.
Chinese journalist after US war briefing, quoted in the *New York Times*, April 2003

General Franks [Iraq war commander] left his successor, General Ricardo Sanchez, with only 27 intelligence officers . . . Bush sent 1,200 intelligence officers and WMD specialists, led by former arms inspector David Kay . . . Kay actually ordered his covert intelligence officers to break off all contact with Iraqi informants who didn't have WMD information, even if they did have information about the insurgency.
Joe Klein, *Politics Lost*

The Earls of Derby and Salisbury happened to be in Spain at the Battle of TARIFA (1340), where Arabs used cannon against the Spaniards. They introduced cannon to the English army, which used them against the French at CRÉCY six years later . . . The Battle of TOWTON (1461) is believed to be the bloodiest ever fought on British soil, with around twenty-eight thousand Lancastrian and Yorkist deaths . . . The Battle of DETTINGEN (1743) was the last when a British sovereign – George II – led his troops in person, and odds of 4-1 against him being killed were offered in London coffee houses . . . At least half the crew of the Victory at TRAFALGAR (1805) were foreign because of chronic recruitment difficulties . . . TEL-EL-KEBIR (1882) was the last battle the British fought in red coats . . . The Battle of KARULA (1904) during the British invasion of Tibet is believed to be the highest ever fought . . . The Battle of the MARNE (1914) saw the first use of motorized infantry – the French rushed out a brigade of reinforcements in two thousand Paris taxis . . . As late as Easter 1916, leave trains from France were stopped for five days so as not to interfere with the holiday traffic . . . In the Pacific War Navajo was used in code because the Japanese could not understand the language . . . When the Japanese were on the brink of capturing SINGAPORE in 1942, the British military wanted to place a strongpoint on the golf course. They were told nothing could be done until the committee had met . . . Isoroku Yamamoto, Grand Admiral of the Imperial Japanese Navy, wore a white uniform almost every day of the war except 18 April 1943, when he was shot down by the US. That day he was wearing khaki . . . In the First World War, 3.5 per cent of the French population died, 2.9 per cent of Germans, 1.9 per cent of British; in the Second World War more than thirty-six million Europeans *died, more than half of them non-combatants: Yugoslavia lost one person in eight, the Soviet Union one in eleven, Germany one in fifteen, Britain one in 125 . . . In VIETNAM only one US soldier in seven was in combat.*

Writing

People think I can teach them style. What stuff it is.
Have something to say and say it as clearly as you can.
That is the only secret of style.
Matthew Arnold

Originality is the art of concealing your source.
Franklin P. Jones

It is one of the paradoxes of writing that, while there is nothing else in the world one would rather do, yet one does anything else in the world to avoid doing it.
Alan Bennett

Everything a writer learns about the art or craft of fiction takes just a little away from his need or drive to write at all. In the end he knows all the tricks and has nothing to say.
Raymond Chandler, quoted in the *Times Literary Supplement*, 1983

Those whom the gods wish to destroy, they first call promising.
Cyril Connolly

He writes like a Pakistani who has learned English when he was twelve years old in order to become a chartered accountant.
John Osborne on G. B. Shaw, quoted in the *Daily Telegraph*, 1994

May I die like a dog rather than hasten by one second a sentence of mine which is not ready.
Gustave Flaubert

A disciplined eye and a wild mind: the main requirements of comedy writing.
Dorothy Parker

Prose consists less and less of *words* chosen for the sake of their meaning, and more and more of *phrases* tacked together like sections of a pre-fabricated henhouse.
George Orwell, *Politics and the English Language*

When . . . I told my father I wanted to be a writer, he had asked me to consider my unfortunate wife, who would have me about the house all day 'wearing a dressing gown, brewing tea and stumped for words'.
John Mortimer, *Murderers and Other Friends*

'If you're from New Jersey,' Nathan said, 'and you write thirty books, and win the Nobel Prize, and you live to be white-haired and ninety-five, it's highly unlikely but not impossible that after your death they'll decide to name a rest stop after you on the Jersey Turnpike. And so, long after you're gone, you may indeed be remembered, but mostly by small children, in the backs of cars, when they lean forward and tell their parents, "Stop, please, stop at Zuckerman – I need to make a pee." For a New Jersey novelist, that's as much immortality as it's realistic to hope for.'
Philip Roth, *The Counterlife*

The only authors who are worthy of the Nobel Prize are those who are impossible to read. It is they who constantly renew the language.
Arthur Lundkvist, Swedish academician, quoted in the *Observer*, 1986

It amazes me to read of the boom of Christopher Hollis, Evelyn Waugh and Peter Quennell because I know I could do much better than they and I don't want the trouble of doing so.

Oxford don Richard Pares, quoted in D. J. Taylor, *On the Corinthian Spirit*

At the height of his career, Henry James told the best-selling Edith Wharton that with the royalties from his previous novel he had managed to buy a wheelbarrow in which to transport his guests' baggage from the railway station, and with the proceeds from the next he hoped to have the vehicle repainted.

***New York Review of Books*, 1997**

The average newspaper reporter writes better English than Henry, if good English means clear, comprehensible English . . . Take any considerable sentence from any of his novels and examine its architecture. Isn't it wobbly with qualifying clauses and subassistant phrases? Doesn't it wriggle and stumble and stagger and flounder? Isn't it 'crude, untidy, careless', bedraggled, loose, frowsy, disorderly, unkempt, uncombed, uncurried, unbrushed, unscrubbed? Doesn't it begin in the middle and work away from both ends? Doesn't it often bounce along for a while and then, of a sudden, roll up its eyes and go out of business entirely?

H. L. Mencken on Henry James, 1905

But what words *exactly* did he use? People who aren't writers never describe things *exactly*.

Iris Murdoch, *The Black Prince*

A visitor, Charles Barbaroux, once called on him [Marat] to find him busy writing. 'He was in a hurry; the printer was calling for copy. You should have seen the casual way in which he composed his articles. Without knowing anything about some public man, he would ask the first person he met what he thought of him and write it down. "I'll ruin the rascal," he would say.'

Christopher Hibbert, *The French Revolution*

It is not enough to succeed. All your friends and contemporaries must fail. Writers are like this even when we try like hell not to be.

Erica Jong, quoted in the *Guardian*, 2000

I love deadlines. I love the whooshing noise they make as they fly by.

Douglas Adams

Dora Russell has now delivered a manuscript on *Religion in the Machine Age* to the publishers Routledge and Kegan Paul, aged 88, having signed the contract in March 1923.

***Guardian*, 1983**

While researching for this biography I came across an old plastic bag filled with little blue diaries. With some excitement I opened one. It read:

> *April 2* – Phlegm
> *April 9* – Paid Sunday papers. Three shillings and
>   ninepence.
> *June 1* – One pill in night.
> *July 23* – Had a Cold
> *September 5* – Phlegm
> *December 19* – Very wet and cold.

I opened another:

> *February 24* – New batteries
> *August 24* – To Exeter
> *December 13* – Very wheezy. One pill night. Improved
>   midday. Went to post.
> *December 17* – Took pill . . . .

Anthony Anderson, *The Man Who Was H. M. Bateman*

A song written in a meadow has the emotion of dandelions. A short story comes out of a hotel room and not a country estate. All great performances begin in a filthy rehearsal room that has pipes running across the ceiling and is one flight over a cheap restaurant.
Jimmy Breslin

Yogi-isms

Sayings attributed to Yogi Berra (b. 1925), baseball player, manager and America's best-loved malapropist:

You better cut the pizza in four pieces. I'm not hungry enough to eat six.

You can observe a lot by watching.

Never answer an anonymous letter.

When you come to a fork in the road, take it.

If the world was perfect, it wouldn't be.

I usually take a two-hour nap from one till four.

Ninety per cent of the game is half mental.

Always go to other people's funerals, otherwise they won't go to yours.

The future ain't what it used to be.

YOGI: Where have you been?
WIFE: I took Tim to see *Dr Zhivago*.
YOGI: What the hell's wrong with him now?

LADY: My, you look mighty cool today.
YOGI: Thank you, ma'am, you don't look so hot yourself.

It ain't over till it's over.

I didn't say everything I said.

The Young

The modern generation, they're all the same.
Give 'em a leg to stand on, they use it to kick you
up the arse.
Minder, ITV (1981)

There are no musts in my life. I'm free, white and
twenty-one.
Film: *I am a Fugitive from a Chain Gang* (1932)

They were members of the first generation to go through
life with no last names.
Tom Wolfe, *I am Charlotte Simmons*

Yer worse than my dad. He's old and he's got an excuse
for being a prick.
Film: *Gregory's Girl* (1981)

In most men, there exists a poet who died young,
whom the man survived.
Augustin de Saint-Beuve

THE LAURIE ENGEL FUND

My son Laurie – who for the first eleven years of his life
never suffered from anything worse than athlete's foot
– died of cancer in September 2005, aged thirteen.

After his death my wife Hilary and I discovered that his
illness formed part of a growing pattern. Cancers in older
children, though still mercifully rare, are increasing.
Non-specialist doctors are, understandably, often slow to
diagnose them. The death rate is higher than it should be.

And even the comparatively lucky patients face long,
debilitating courses of treatment that blight their young
lives. All too often, they will spend years in inappropriate
hospital wards – either alongside infants or dumped in
with the geriatrics. Laurie was treated in the Birmingham
Children's Hospital, where the care was world-class but
the facilities dire.

So we began raising funds for Teenage Cancer Trust,
who build specialist units for teenagers to improve both
their medical care and their enjoyment of life. Our aim
was to help improve the ward at Birmingham, a centre of
excellence that treats children from all over the country,
to create a new TCT unit and ensure future patients have
an easier time than Laurie did.

By the end of 2006 the fund had raised more than
£400,000 towards this project, way beyond our wildest

dreams. TCT and hospital officials were hoping building work would start in early 2007, so that teenagers could start getting the benefit before the end of the year.

All the royalties from this book (a more generous deal than normal in publishing) will go towards the Laurie Engel Fund. For more details, for a copy of Hilary's book, *LAURIE: The Boy Who Lived*, or to make a donation:

Please log on to	www.laurieengelfund.org
e-mail	tctlaurie1@aol.com
or write to	TCT Laurie Engel Fund,
	Fair Oak,
	Bacton,
	Herefordshire
	HR2 0AT

For Teenage Cancer Trust
(registered charity No. 1062559)

log on to	www.teenagecancertrust.org
or call	020 7612 0370.

Matthew Engel

Laurie-isms

Mummy, if you don't get up and make me a drink, I won't say you're pretty any more.
Age three

I want my Robin costume on, Mum. You know you can do it. You're a big girl, ain'tcha?
Age four

God rules the world. Jeremy told me.
Age four

LAURIE: What am I doing today?
MUM: You're going to school.
LAURIE: What? AGAIN?
Second day of school

Why do you hate change? Change is money.
To his father, age five

I'm a vegetarian but I eat meat.
Age six

MUM: When we move to our new house, you'll be able to camp by the stream.
LAURIE: I think if you pay £365,000 for a house, you really ought to use it.
Age seven

MUM (sitting in the back of the car): Oh, there's a child
    lock. I can't get out.
LAURIE: Welcome to *my* world.
Age eight

Deep in the darkness a shadow lingers
Reaching out with its merciless fingers
This is a creature that doesn't have feelings
This creature does not accept appealing.
But through the evil of the earth
Lies a land of hope and rebirth
Where the land is made of honey and milk
Where the flowers grow brightly and the clothes are silk.
This land is known as the Republic of Heaven,
Ruled by God and His angels seven.
Here death may not enter,
Death may not fight,
For this is the land of good and of light.
Poem, age nine

Dear school,
    I am going into Birmingham for my second round of
chemotherapy tomorrow and quite frankly, I'd rather
spend the eight weeks doing non-stop maths homework
while hanging upside down from a flaming tree.
Letter, age twelve

Sleep. Tomorrow will bring the sun . . .

Lullaby, age seven

This quotation has been inscribed on Laurie's gravestone